D1621800

THE SOUTHERN
COAST-TO-COAST WALK

Gibbet Hill, Hindhead

THE SOUTHERN COAST-TO-COAST WALK

by

Ray Quinlan

CICERONE PRESS
MILNTHORPE, CUMBRIA

© Ray Quinlan 1993
ISBN 1 85284 117 6
British Library Cataloguing-in-Publication Data.
A catalogue record for this book is available from the British Library.

To Tilly
who would do the walk
if she only had the time

Other Cicerone book by Ray Quinlan :

THE KENNET & AVON WALK

CONTENTS

KEY TO MAPS

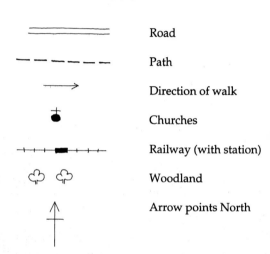

	Road
	Path
	Direction of walk
	Churches
	Railway (with station)
	Woodland
	Arrow points North

Advice to Readers

Readers are advised that whilst every effort is taken by the author to ensure the accuracy of this guidebook, changes can occur which may affect the contents. It is advisable to check locally on transport, accommodation, shops etc but even rights-of-way can be altered and, more especially overseas, paths can be eradicated by landslip, forest fires or changes of ownership.

The publisher would welcome notes of any such changes

INTRODUCTION

I walked from Sandgate to Folkestone with a local man who was just out for an afternoon stroll. We'd both been drenched by a sudden rush of the high tide; one of those small events that help break the traditional British reserve. Naturally, it was only a matter of time before he asked the inevitable question:

"So where have you walked from?"

A spark of mischievous delight shot through my mind and back came the, admittedly facetious, reply:

"From Weston-super-Mare."

"Oh," he said with the kind of knowing look that I should imagine psychiatrists don before committing somebody to an institution. "I think," he continued, "we'd better get a move on before it rains."

This book, which describes a Southern Coast to Coast Walk, is an attempt to show that although the south will never rival the north for dramatic mountain landscape it can still produce a fine long-distance pathway. It is a suggested route along a number of established and waymarked, but perhaps less well known, long-distance paths joined together by lines of my own. Incorporated within this route are: the West Mendip Way, most of the proposed East Mendip Way, part of the Imber Range Path, most of the Clarendon Way, part of the Itchen Way, virtually the entire Greensand Way and part of the Saxon Shore Path. Using these stepping stones, we start at Weston-super-Mare and pass over the Mendip Hills to Wells. From there, we go north of Shepton Mallet to Frome and Warminster and then along the Wylye Valley to Salisbury. From Winchester, we follow the River Itchen and then cross the Hampshire Hills to reach Selborne and Hindhead. We then scale the Surrey Hills to the south of Dorking and Reigate to enter Kent where we bypass Westerham and Sevenoaks before arriving at Yalding. The path now winds through Pluckley and Great Chart to skirt Hamstreet and join the Royal Military Canal. The rest of our way follows the coast to Hythe and Folkestone and then on to finish at the tercentenary plaque near the Hoverport at Dover: 283 miles from the Grand Pier at Weston.

I've described the route in sixty sections of four to six miles. These divisions were made for reasons of geography and space rather than as recommended excursions. Different individuals will want to walk the route in different ways and the aim of the format is to let you plan your own schedule. Suggested itineraries are given in Appendix 1 and there I suggest that strong walkers who wish to undertake the walk in one "bash" could do it in just over a fortnight. Others of a more plodding stride, like myself, might prefer to stretch it out for another week. Either way, we are not in a race and there's plenty to see.

The text describes the route in detail but describing 283 miles in sixty pages does lead to succinctness. Please note that R = right; L = left, a T-jct is a T-junction and a X-path or X-track is a cross-path or cross-track. Pubs recommended in the Campaign for Real Ale's *Good Pub Guide 1993* are denoted (CAMRA). Pubs recommended by the *Good Pub Guide 1993* (ed. by Alisdair Aird, Ebury Press) are denoted (GPG). The approximate length of each section is described in brackets at the bottom of the text (m = miles; km = kilometres). The maps are strictly hand-drawn, sketch maps and are designed to illustrate the text rather than the countryside. The route is marked with a series of dashes and the direction indicated with arrows. The maps are not accurate enough to be definitive! For more detail of both the route and its surroundings (and to check the course of a right of way), Ordnance Survey maps are recommended. The appropriate map number for each section of the walk is described in brackets at the bottom of each text section. OSL = Ordnance Survey Landranger (1:50,000) series. OSP = Ordnance Survey Pathfinder (1:25,000) series.

The route follows rights of way or permissive paths throughout as checked with local authority rights of way departments. Only in Somerset did I find problems with officially designated paths being blocked on the ground. This situation will remedy itself with the establishment of the East Mendip Way, a project supported by Somerset County Council which will soon be blessed with new stiles and waymark notices. In some places along this new route alterations to the present rights of way are planned. The walker should therefore keep an eye open for (and follow the advice of) waymarks between Shepton Mallet and the Perimeter Path just north of Chantry (where the EMW goes south and we go north to visit the fine village of Mells).

Walkers should, of course, be prepared on any walk for poor weather and adverse underfoot conditions. I was blessed with a drought ridden winter and so came through relatively unscathed. However, mud was still prevalent and trainers would not have been adequate footwear. You may also be surprised how often there are large gaps between suitable refreshment stops en route. Where possible, I have indicated where pubs and shops are available but normally it would be sensible to carry something to eat and drink with you.

Difficult bits? Well there's a surprising amount of "up" involved in the Mendips and on the Surrey Hills. I also won't forget the four to five foot leap down a groyne near Sandgate when the tide was in. Otherwise none really. It's an easy, trouble free route that should be within the capacity of most weekend walkers. However, I wish I had a pound for every dog that rushed up and barked at me and I'll never forget the two hours I spent on Ludshott Common apparently going round in circles. In the absence of such hazards, I trust that you will enjoy the walk.

Weston-Super-Mare. Section 1

Swimming pool, Weston-Super-Mare. Section 1

Over the Mendip Hills

They call it Weston-super-Mud; rather unfairly I think. Weston has a vast expanse of sand, a pleasant outlook to Flat Holm and Steep Holm, all the amusements you'd expect in a British seaside resort and what the guidebook calls a "mild but bracing climate". As it is also the start of this Southern Coast to Coast Walk what more could it need? Those who do the walk in season can set off from the end of the Grand Pier. Those like me, who seem to visit such places when they are shut, can begin near the "Trespassers Will Be Prosecuted" notices. Either way it's 283 miles to Dover which is a lot of small steps or giant leaps for anyone.

The West Mendip Way starts in rather inauspicious surroundings at the entrance to a boat-yard in Uphill. Why the founders of the route, a confederation of local Rotary Clubs, decided to start here rather than on the Weston esplanade I don't know but we follow the WMW for just over thirty miles to Wells. The intervening land is fine walking country. The hills aren't high by northern standards (the highest, Black Down, is just 325 metres) but they offer splendid views to the Bristol Channel, the peat bogs of Sedgemoor and the tor at Glastonbury. The route over Compton Hill and Wavering Down follows a high, airy ridge away from the seemingly ubiquitous noise and bustle of Southern England. It's invigorating stuff.

That noise and bustle, of course, is as much a part of Cheddar and Wells as it is of the cities to the north. Go to either in summer and you'll meet the crowds head on. They come to see the spectacular limestone scenery and to visit the eerie caves and grottoes of Cheddar and Wookey Hole. Coast to coasters can visit the towering cliffs of Cheddar Gorge as well as the caves by turning right after going through Black Rock Nature Reserve (section 4). A second opportunity to see this type of landscape arises a few miles further on when the walk goes through Ebbor Gorge and passes the entrance to the Wookey Hole caves.

The WMW ends at Wells: a packed little town even out of season but with a good deal of charm for all that. It's worth making a diversion to see the cathedral which sports one of the most impressive faces of any in the country, decorated as it is with 400 statues of various saints, angels and prophets. The Southern Coast to Coast leaves Wells via the Bishops Palace precinct and heads to the east Mendip. Although we are leaving the high hills and deep gorges behind, the country still has great appeal and a wild and lonely flavour. Our only brush with bustle between Wells and Frome comes as we skirt the northern fringes of Shepton Mallet and even then it is the acceptable, amiable face of civilisation that confronts us. The gentleness of the countryside around here has been recognised by David Wright of Frome College who plans to establish the East Mendip Way. Our only diversion from the proposed route takes us to the charming village of Mells and then along the Wadbury Valley. Here the remains of Fussell's Iron Works will entertain the industrial archaeologist while the rest of us simply take in the wonder of this watery chasm before undertaking the somewhat less entertaining plod into Frome.

The first opportunity for refreshment on this section (from a pub or a shop en route) is at Shipham. It's therefore a good idea to stock up at Weston before setting off. Further on, Cheddar is close enough ($^1/_2$ mile to R from Bradley Cross) to visit for both provisions and accommodation. Draycott has both a pub and a small shop whereas Priddy is blessed with two pubs: the New Inn and the Queen Victoria (both GPG). Wookey Hole has a range of facilities (the Burcott Inn is CAMRA/GPG) and Wells is a positive metropolis compared with anything met so far. Shepton Mallet also has a number of shops and pubs (the Horseshoe Inn and Kings Arms are both CAMRA). Between there and Frome, good planning is again required as facilities are limited to a pub at Chelynch and both a pub and a shop at Mells. Frome is Wells size and has everything for the next phase of the walk: Wiltshire.

Priddy. Section 5

1: WESTON-SUPER-MARE

The walk starts at the Grand Pier. Face the sea and turn L to go along the promenade. At the end continue on the beach until the dunes L subside and you reach a road. Walk up the road towards the hilltop Uphill Old Church. At the base of the rock, turn R into Uphill Boat Centre. Go through the yard and bear L through a gate into a nature reserve. Go through an old quarry into a field. As a clear path runs up a slope, bear R towards Walborough tumulus. Go over a stile and round the edge of the mound without losing height. At a waymark post, turn R onto a dyke. Just before a gate, turn L over a stile. Go straight across a field to a further stile which leads over a brook via a plank. In the next field, turn L through a gate into a narrow field. The path becomes more distinct and eventually goes R through a gate and then L to reach the A370. Turn R, over a railway and along the road, to reach a turning signposted for parking. Turn L to go along the old road to a farmyard. Just after the farm buildings, turn L up the unmetalled Purn Lane. Near the top go R through a gate and descend to a narrow path with high hedging. When this opens out, take the path that goes L and then R to an open field and a slurry tank. Go round the tank and back onto the path to a stile next to a gate. Cross a second stile into an alley with houses to R. Cross four stiles to reach allotments and a gate. As the main path bends R, go straight over a stile to a field. Bear L but keep the hedge close R. Cross a stile beneath some bungalows. Keep the fence close R to go through a gate. Now keep the wall close L to reach a ladder stile and a minor road. Cross the road to a driveway and turn immediately L to go up hill to a stile and a hedged path. After another stile, bear L across a field to a sparse hedge with a path running along the centre of it. Turn R and go uphill to cross a stile. Bear R with a hedge R to a field and up a shallow valley towards the telegraph pole on the horizon. Cross a stile into a road and turn R.

(OSL 182: OSP 1181/1197) (5.25m/8.25km)

START 1: WESTON-SUPER-MARE,

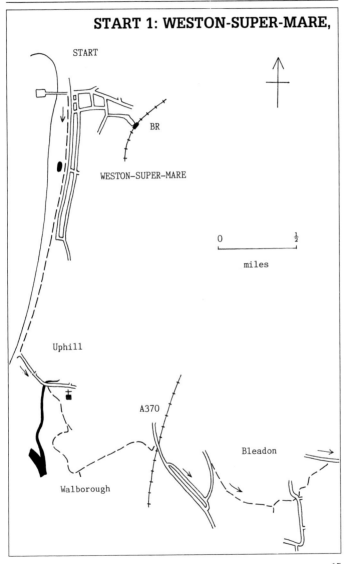

START

BR

WESTON–SUPER–MARE

0 ————————— ½

miles

Uphill

A370

Bleadon

Walborough

2: LOXTON

Walk along the road, past Gracelands, for about a mile with fine views of Loxton Hill R. Just after Shiplett Hill Farm, the road turns abruptly L. Here continue straight on along an unmetalled lane which soon turns into a path and passes through light wood and hedging to a T-jct. Turn R up a lane for about 100yds and then R again at another junction. Take the next L turn (as indicated by a waymark post), through a gate and up on to Loxton Hill. The clear path now runs straight for about $1^{1}/_{4}$ miles. There are fine views L to Crook Peak and Compton Hill. The path comes out to an unmetalled lane. Turn R into Hillview Road then go downhill to North Lodge and into Loxton. Turn R and then L along Church Road following signs for Loxton Church. At the end of this road, follow footpath signs R into a farmyard. Bear L to reach a gate. The path heads across the field in the direction of the motorway bridge to an electricity sub-station. Cross the stile and turn R to go through a gate and out to a minor road. Turn L to cross the M5 and go past the Wheelright's Shop and Museum. Turn L along Barton Road, signposted to Winscombe. After passing The Lodge and The Paddock, you will come to an area of roadside parking and a footpath which runs R up through the trees. This easy to follow path, twists through the undergrowth to climb up to the side of Crook Peak. Continue along the clear line with the peak to the R. This leads to a point where the path meets two walls that join one another at right angles. Bear L here so that the wall is to your L. There is now a superb view down the hill to the south-east of the village of Compton Bishop and east towards the next of the Mendip Hills, Wavering Down. The path follows the ridge over Compton Hill and on to Wavering Down. Keep the wall close L for the whole 2 miles.

(OSL 182: OSP 1197) (5.25m/8.25km)

2: LOXTON

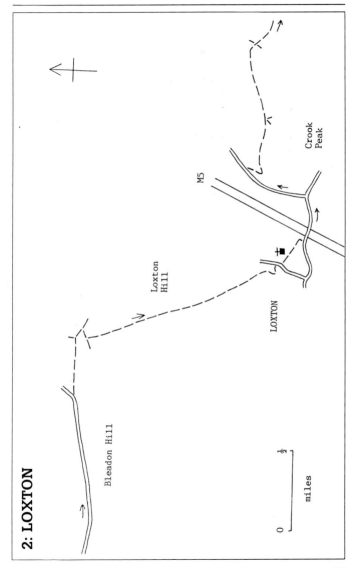

Crook Peak

M5

Loxton Hill

LOXTON

Bleadon Hill

miles

0   ½

3: SHIPHAM

With the wall still close L, the path goes over Wavering Down to a trig point and then the wonderfully positioned Hill Farm. Eventually, the path enters Kings Wood and descends to the A38. From the gate and car park that mark the bottom of Wavering Down and Kings Wood, turn R to pass along a minor road to reach the A38 near a bus stop. Turn L and, just before a service station, go R up a path into woodland. Continue straight avoiding paths off to R until you reach a farm gate (for a track going straight on) and a footpath sign pointing R. Contrarily turn L to enter Winscombe Drove which immediately bends R. This muddy track continues for just under a mile before descending into a slight hollow and then rising again to meet a turning off L. Take this turning and, before reaching the buildings of Winterhead Hill Farm, turn R through a gate. Take a straight course across the field to a stile marked clearly with a white arrow. Continue into the next field and keep the hedge close L. After 200yds the path descends rapidly to a small stream with stepping stones. Cross and take the path up to a minor road at Shipham. (Turn L here for a small shop and the Miners Arms.) To continue the walk, turn R for 20-30yds and then L along Templar's Way. Follow this lane into the drive of Hilltop Meadow and then past the house to a metal gate next to a farm gate. Follow the clear path through low woodland out to an open area. Carry straight on at a waymark post to another post next to a fence. Walk on for 10yds and then bear L downhill along a dirt drive (with views of Weston to L). The drive bends R to go L of a barn and then descends between hedges to a pink house and a lane (Lippiatt Lane). Turn R.

(OSL 182: OSP 1198) (4.25m/6.5km)

3: SHIPHAM

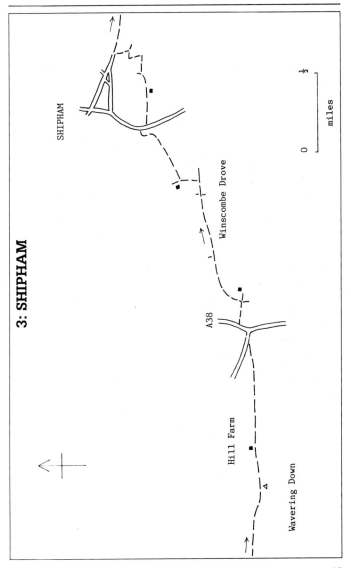

SHIPHAM

Winscombe Drove

A38

Hill Farm

Wavering Down

0 — ½ miles

4: CHEDDAR

At the end of the lane, continue along a muddy track into woods.
Enter Rowberrow Warren and, at the bottom of the hill, turn R.
Cross a stream and bear L up a clear track to reach a forest drive.
Bear R and, after $^{1}/_{3}$ mile, go over a cross track and along a path that
leaves the warren. Go along the fenced path, past some stables at
Tynings, to a road. Turn L for $^{2}/_{3}$ mile before going R along a drive
to Pineysleight and Charterhouse Farms. At the farm, bear R
around the buildings to a gate in a stone wall. Turn L to walk with
the wall (and then a hedge) R to a gate and a stile. Cross this and go
downhill through woods. At the bottom, cross a stile into Black
Rock Nature Reserve. Walk through the quarry along a path which
winds around the rock face and out over two stiles to the B3135 at
the top of Cheddar Gorge. Bear R to a path which climbs steeply
through woods. At the top, go R for 50-100yds to an indistinct fork.
Bear L to a wall and then R for 50yds to a stile. Cross this and bear
R away from the wall with fine views ahead. A grassy path now
descends towards Cheddar. At a X-track, turn R to continue downhill
with an area of woods to L. When this thins, turn L along a fenced
path (with a golf driving range R) and through a gate. The narrow
path curves around the edge of a hill to a T-jct. Turn R and then L
along a metalled drive which descends to Bradley Cottage (L). Just
past this house, go L up a dirt drive, through a gate and uphill to a
waymark post. Continue along a gully. At the top go through a gate
into the next field and then follow the track as it bends L to go
through a gate. Continue along a path and through another gate.
Bear L uphill with a farm to R. In the next field walk on with a wall
close R. Go through two gates and bear R over pasture to a waymark
post. Here turn R to go downhill to the L of a dew pond and on with
Batcombe Hollow to R.

(OSL 182: OSP 1198) (6.5m/10.5km)

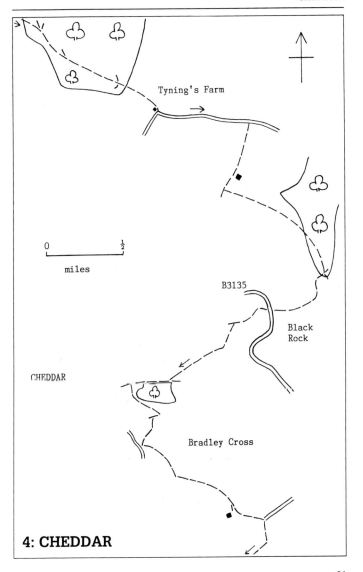

Tyning's Farm

B3135

Black
Rock

CHEDDAR

Bradley Cross

miles

0   ½

4: CHEDDAR

5: DRAYCOTT

The path goes round hairpin bends and over a stile. Follow the clear route which goes through Batcombe Farmyard (to L of main buildings). Once through the yard, walk on to the farm drive and bear L to a road. Turn L to walk into Draycott. Go past the Red Lion and a small shop. Turn L near a small monument and the village pump. This lane goes uphill to reach a dirt path and a stile near a gate. Continue straight on with fence and hedge R. After crossing the next stile, bear R slightly to go over two stiles (both marked in yellow) and then continue along the R edge of the field. After passing a small beech copse, cross the next three fields by following along a similar course. After going over a double stile, bear R to walk along the R edge of the field. Now cross two stiles to a road. Go straight on along a lane. When this jinks L, cross a stile R and head over the field to another stile to R of a clear gate on the horizon. Follow the same diagonal course to cross a stile in the far corner of the next field. Turn R along a road and walk on to reach Priddy Village Green. Bear R, past the New Inn and then turn R to pass the Queen Victoria Inn. Continue along the road for $^1/_3$ mile to turn L over a stile. Walk on with wall close L to the corner of the field and then turn R to go over a stile in the opposite corner. Walk into the next field with a wall to L. Halfway along, cross a stile so that you continue on with the wall now to R. Follow the R edge of this field as it bends L and around to a stile into a green lane. Turn L and walk on to pass a gate (R) after which follow the main drive R and along the well-marked route through Higher Pitts Farm. Leave the farm via a gate. Follow the R edge of the field into the next field with good views ahead. Follow the fence around R to cross a stile into Ebbor Gorge National Nature Reserve. Bear L downhill to cross a stile. Now turn L into woods and follow the clear path (signposted for the car park) through the gorge.

(OSL 182: OSP 1198/1218) (6.5m/10.5km)

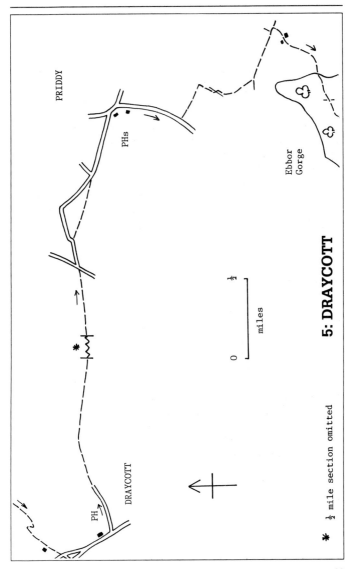

PRIDDY

PHs

Ebbor
Gorge

5: DRAYCOTT

0 miles ½

DRAYCOTT

PH

* ½ mile section omitted

6: WELLS

The path descends through woods. At a T-jct, turn L along the valley bottom eventually to reach a road. Turn L and walk into Wookey Hole. Follow the main road through the village to pass the entrance to the caves and the Wookey Hole Inn. After passing Milton Lane (L), go L through a kissing gate. Walk uphill with a hedge R. This bends R to another gate and a fenced path. After the next kissing gate, turn L and ascend the hill (Arthur's Point) with views back to Ebbor Gorge. Bear R over the summit and then turn R to descend to a stile and a field. Turn L to follow the hedge to a gate into an old quarry. Go ahead along the metalled lane which bends L (with main quarry area to R) to a road. Turn R for 250yds. When the main lane bends L, go straight along a signposted footpath which starts at a kissing gate. Follow the alley across two roads to a school. Continue along a similar course to take a path that runs between playing fields. At the end turn L along Lover's Walk and then R and L to reach a road (note the West Mendip Way plaque on wall to L). Turn R and go straight on at the roundabout to take the next L turn (Sadler St). After passing the Swan Hotel, turn L to reach the precincts of the Bishops Palace via the huge gate to R of the National Trust shop. Turn R and walk on with the palace and moat to L. At the end, go past Islington Cottage onto a path signposted to Dulcote. After $^2/_3$ mile, cross a road to go through a gate (signposted to Dunder). Walk on to another gate with a pill box high to L. The path follows the R edge of the next field to a green lane. Turn L uphill through woods to a stile. Follow the L hedge to a gate and a wide track. Turn R and follow the track to a gate into King's Castle Wood Nature Reserve. The path now bends L to a T-jct. Turn R. The worn path goes over grassland following a roughly straight course, through a gate and along the L edge of a field.

(OSL 182: OSP 1198/1218) (5.25m/8.5km)

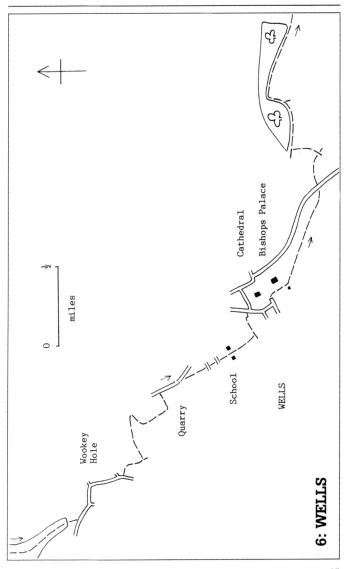

6: WELLS

THE SOUTHERN COAST-TO-COAST

7: SHEPTON MALLET

Continue to a gate and a drive. Turn R through the second gate R and bear L with a pill box R. Head towards the R corner of the field to go through a gate and along a grassy path to a field, a gate and a lane. Turn L. After 300yds go R over a stile across a narrow field and over another stile. Bear L to the top L corner. Go through two gates and on with a hedge close L. At a road turn L and, after 200yds, R over a stile. Bear L through two hedge gaps to reach a stile in the corner of the next field. Follow the hedge R until it turns R. Bear slightly R to a stile into the next field. Go across the middle of this field, through an open hedge and on over a stile into woods. Follow a clear path to a quarry. Here go L and then R up steps to a stile and the top of the cliff. Turn L to follow the field edge to a stile and a lane. Turn R and, after 10yds, L along a hedged path (Rubble Lane) to a lane. Turn L for ¹/₃ mile and then R onto an old railway embankment. Walk along this until you reach gates. Turn R to go over two stiles and then follow the hedge down to a third. The path now goes L between houses to a minor road. Bear R to go along a narrow alley to a busier road. Cross this road and bear R to go up some steps. Cross a stile and turn R to the far hedge. Now turn L to reach an old railway embankment. Turn R, over a stile and walk on with railway L. After ¹/₄ mile, the path bears R to go under the embankment and out to a road. Turn R for 100 yds and then L along Great Barton. Follow this alley round to go under Charlton Railway Viaduct. Turn R to a stile into a field. Walk on with a wall close L to a stile. Go over the stile and across the field, past a redundant stile, to reach a stone stile into a green lane. Cross this (Fosse Way) and the stile opposite. Now bear L to go through an orchard to the top L corner. Go through a stile, across a lane and over another stile to walk uphill with a hedge close R.

(OSL 183: OSP 1218/1219) (5m/8km)

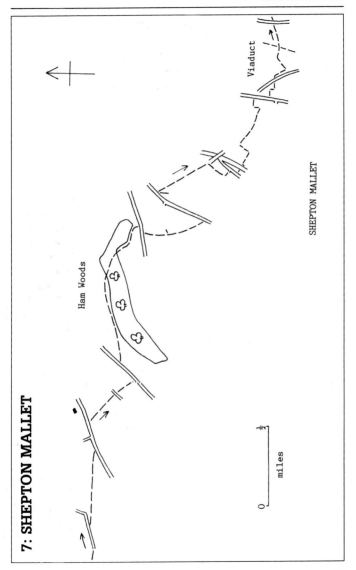

7: SHEPTON MALLET

Ham Woods

Viaduct

SHEPTON MALLET

miles

8: CHELYNCH

Cross a stile to walk up Ingsdons Hill. Continue on this course with hedge L to a gravel drive. When this goes L, go straight on with hedge R. Go over a stile and on eventually to cross a stile to a lane. Turn R. At a T-jct, turn L to pass The Poachers Pocket. At the road junction, go L and walk on to overhead power lines. Here turn R up some steps into a field. Cross towards a trough and then turn L to follow the wall. At the end of the field, go through the hedge and on along a row of trees to a stile and then a gate into a lane. Turn R and, after a few yds, L through a gate. (NB. Right of Way changes are planned here so watch for signposts.) Bear R up a slope with a fence R. When this bends R go straight on to a stile. Follow a similar line over the next field to cross a stile and on with a farm to L to a stile and a road. Turn L and then R along a lane. At a road, bear L up a dirt drive with a wall R. When the wall ends turn R up a track. Cross a metal fence and walk on to a hedge gap. Bear R over the next field and, with hedge L, continue to a gate (L). Go through this and on to skirt the corner of the field to R. Follow the same course to go over a gate. Go through some undergrowth and turn L to a dirt drive. Turn R, past a house, to go through a gate with woods R. After going through two gates and over a stile, turn L up a hedged path with Cranmore Tower to R. Continue through a gate with conifers L. At the end of the wood where the path bears L, turn R along a broad track and through a gate. Bear R into a wood. Go over a major X-track and round to reach a farm gate L. Cross a stile and immediately bear L away from the more obvious drive to follow a similar course but with hedge R. Follow this round and through a gate onto a dirt drive that passes underground reservoirs. Before entering a farmyard, go L, over a stile, and walk on with fence and house R to the far corner of the field and a road.

(OSL 183: OSP 1219) (4.75m/7.5km)

8: CHELYNCH

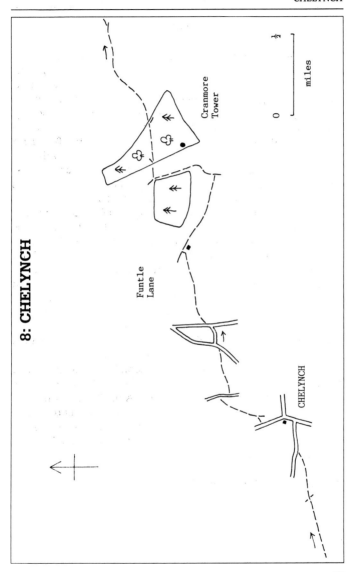

Cranmore Tower

Funtle Lane

CHELYNCH

0   ½

miles

9: MELLS

Walk straight on along the road until it bends L near The Old School. Here bear R along a driveway. When the lane goes L to a bungalow, go straight on over a stile. Follow the L edge of the field to a dead end. Here the right of way goes over the barbed wire fence. Follow the clear path which runs along a valley bottom through woods (a Somerset Trust for Nature Conservation Reserve). Cross a small stream and, after 10yds, go R at a fork. This path leads to a T-jct. Turn R and continue through rivers of mud to a lane. Turn L to reach Rock House Farm and a road. Turn R and walk on to pass the last bungalow on the L. Here turn L through the gate of Greystones Farm and over pasture towards farm buildings. At the hedge turn R and continue through a gap, across a small field and over a stile. In the next field, head half R towards a livestock shelter. Cross the next field to R of shelter to a gate and a lane. Turn L and then, after 25yds, R through a gate. Turn L to walk with a hedge close L for $^2/_3$ mile. Just before some farm buildings and a pond, cross a stile R and bear R to a further stile. Keep ahead with the quarry still to R over two more stiles. Cross a third into woodland and a fourth into a field. Bear R along a distinct track which follows cables to a broken stile L and a road. Turn R for 10yds and L over a stile. Descend to a hedge and turn R with the hedge to L (this right of way is not marked on OS). Just before the hedge turns L, go L over a stile and descend with hedge to R. Go over a stile and walk on to cross a bridge over Mells Stream to Mells Post Office (turn L for The Talbot Inn). Turn R and bear L along the road to Great Elms. After 300yds, turn R past a gate along a bridleway which follows Mells Stream into a gorge. Pass to the L of an old iron works (go R to investigate first!) and continue on to a drive near Tree Tops. Continue on the path which runs along the L bank of the river.

(OSL 183: OSP 1219) (4.75m/7.5km)

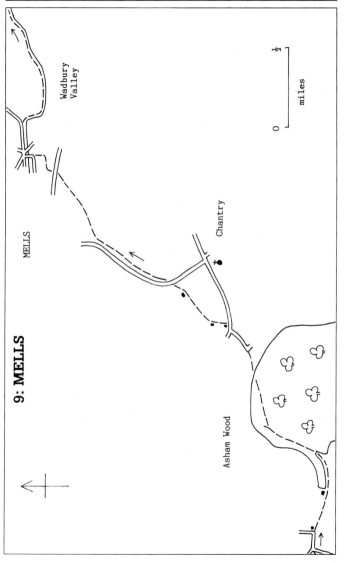

9: MELLS

MELLS

Wadbury
Valley

Chantry

Asham Wood

½

0

miles

10: FROME

Eventually the path rises away from the river to a road. Go straight on and down hill. Cross the river via the road bridge and turn L along a track (the Vallis Vale permissive path) which runs along the R bank of the river. Follow this round, staying on the main path, to go under a bridge and over a footbridge. Go straight on with the river to R; forking R at one point to stay with the river. Don't cross the first footbridge but take the second and follow the path that runs straight on from the bridge to follow another stream into woods. This path passes an old quarry to reach a lane. Go straight on and turn first L. This lane runs for $^1/_2$ mile to a road (Broadway). Turn L and walk into central Frome. Bear R at a roundabout and, after passing some shops and almost opposite a petrol station, bear L down a small lane. This goes past Phoenix Terrace and High Street. Turn L at a bookshop to descend to Market Place. Continue past the post office and over a river bridge. Turn R along Willow Vale with the River Frome R. The lane becomes a private road and goes under an old railway bridge. Continue along the path. At a fork, bear R with houses on hill to L. The path soon rejoins the river and goes under railway bridges. Stay close to the river, bearing R to reach a road junction. Turn L and take the second L turning (Styles Hill A3098). Walk up the hill and take the second R (Styles Avenue). Go to the end of the road to cross the railway and then a new road. Go over the stile and straight across the field to a gap in the hedge. Now bear L to go L of a pylon. Cross a fence and go on in the direction of a church (All Saints, Rodden). Go over a stile and walk around the R side of the church to a farm gate. Go through this and bear L over a field.

(OSL 183: OSP 1219) (4.5m/7km)

Uphill Old Church

Cathedral and Bishop's Palace, Wells

Fields above Wylye

Mill and church at Fisherton de la Mere

10: FROME

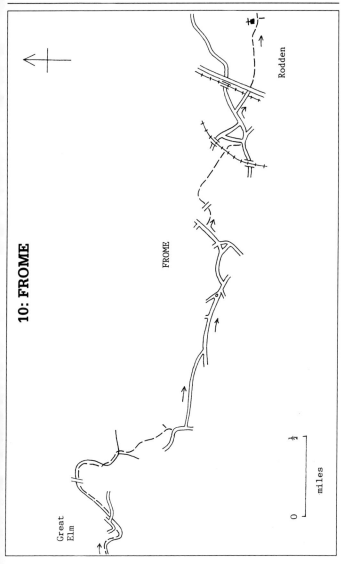

Great
Elm

FROME

Rodden

0 ——— ½
miles

11: CHAPMANSLADE

Go through a gap in the hedge and over the next field, bearing L of a solitary oak. Cross a pair of simple stiles with an intervening railway sleeper bridge into the next field. The right of way bears L into the top L corner of the field. Cross a new stile and walk on to go over a fence and down hill bearing L towards the hedge L. Go over two stiles and up the hill, keeping the hedge close L. Go through a gate to reach and cross another stile. Go through the barbed wire fence into the next field and follow the L edge round to a house. Just beyond turn L to follow the track to a road. Turn R along the road. About 200yds after passing a sign announcing the Wiltshire border, turn L over a stile. The path leads to a second stile and a path which goes R along the edge of a wood. This leads to a stile and a field with fine views L. Go straight on and over the next stile and field to a further stile into a fenced track. Turn R and then, almost immediately, L to a gate. Bear R over a stile and carry on over the next stile. Go straight on through the nursery until the main track turns L. Here go R through the hedge to a stile and then diagonally across the field to two stiles and a road. Cross to a simple stile and continue on the same bearing to another stile which brings you to a road. Turn R to reach the main A36. Bear R and turn L along a road signposted to Thoulstone Park Nursery. Pass the nursery and, as the road bends R, go straight to enter an old drover's lane. Follow this clear track for just over a mile.

(OSL 183: OSP 1220) (4m/6.25km)

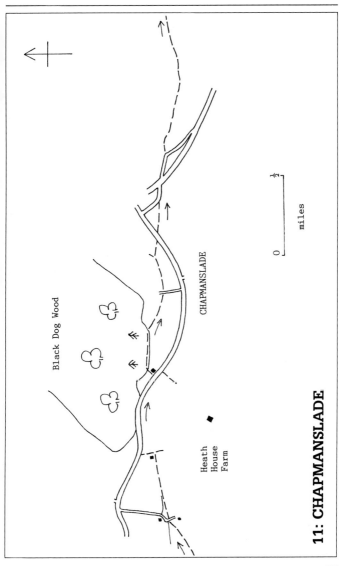

Black Dog Wood

CHAPMANSLADE

Heath
House
Farm

0   ½   miles

11: CHAPMANSLADE

Meel. Section 9

And Across the Wiltshire Plains

Wiltshire is the ultimate curate's egg. Just as you start thinking that here is the wildest and most wonderful county in the whole of Southern England, a gang of helicopters buzz around your ears, a jet drowns out your mental conversation and resounding booms from the nearby firing ranges shake the very ground you're standing on. This, one of the least populated counties in Central Southern England, is for that reason one of the army's favourite spots for a day out. Nowhere is this fact better seen than around the appropriately named Warminster. Here the Southern Coast to Coast joins the southern part of the Imber Range Perimeter Path: a thirty-mile circular walk around the local military playground. On a good day, all is peaceful and relaxing, a perfect antidote to modern living. On a bad day, the walk will be undertaken to a continuous background of tanks roaring up and down the hills and numerous miscellaneous explosions.

And yet Wiltshire could be heaven! This large, comparatively empty, county is dominated by the vast expanse of chalk downland that forms Salisbury Plain. On this herb-rich turf, man has lived for thousands of years and many of our most celebrated ancient sites are to be found here: Avebury Stone Circle, Silbury Hill, the West Kennet Long Barrow and, of course the most famous of all, Stonehenge. Our route, which passes to the north of Warminster and along the southern edge of the Plain, crosses a series of amazingly positioned prehistoric hillforts that provide fine, and presumably defendable, views to the south. It's superb open country and good, easy hill walking. From the Plain we descend into the rural tranquillity of the Wylye Valley at Heytesbury and then continue on to the almost idyllic village of Wylye itself. Now we pass out of the reach of the tanks and head towards Salisbury along an ancient road, the Ox Drove. Here, an hour's walk from the road to Wylye and still an hour from Wilton, I passed the only person I met along the entire six miles of the drove: an old man with a zimmer frame. How he got there, where he was going and whether he made it I'll never know. I was so surprised to see him that I simply forgot to ask.

Wilton was once the capital of all Wessex and although the traffic and buildings come as a bit of a shock after a whole morning of nothing but countryside, it's a pleasant place for luncheon. The Italianate church looks strangely out of place for Wiltshire but the rest is in perfect keeping. Wilton House, home of the Earls of Pembroke, can be found on the other side of the small town and is open for visitors in the appropriate season.

Sadly, there's no easy route from Wilton to Salisbury but the way along the Town Path is as fine an entrance into a city as you'll find, a great view of the famous cathedral. I liked Salisbury. It's interesting yet functional, worth visiting yet not overtly touristy. Walking through it is certainly no hardship and strangely untaxing for those who, like me, don't enjoy pavement plods.

Frome offers a range of shops and pubs at which to draw refreshment. The next opportunity for so doing is the Angel Inn at Upton Scudamore. Warminster is about $^1/_2$ mile south of the Southern Coast to Coast - turn R after the West Wilts Golf Club. The town has a small but adequate shopping centre and a number of hostelries (GPG lists the Old Bell). The next shop is at Wylye. There are however a series of pubs along the way: at Heytesbury (Angel (GPG) & Red Lion), Stockton and Wylye (the Bell is CAMRA & GPG). The stretch from Wylye to Wilton is guaranteed shop and pub free but Wilton and Salisbury have plenty of both. Wilton has the Bear Inn (CAMRA) and Salisbury has the Haunch of Venison & the Red Lion (both CAMRA & GPG).

Mill at Wylye. Section 15

12: WARMINSTER

The drover's track eventually reaches a road junction. Go roughly straight on along a lane signposted to Upton Scudamore. Follow the lane round to pass the church. The lane then bends R (if thirsty turn L here to reach the Angel Inn) and descends to the busy A350. Cross the road and go through a gap in the fence to walk along an old road. When this reaches a road in use, turn L and walk uphill for 250yds. Just as the road starts to bend R, turn R up a wide dirt track which goes uphill to reach an underground reservoir. Go straight on, with a fence to L, onto West Wilts golf course. Keep the fence close L to reach a T-jct. Turn R and follow the path (still with fence close L) round for about $2/3$ mile to the entrance to the golf club. Turn L. Walk on for about 400yds and turn R down Elm Hill. Follow this nearly straight road to the end and turn L at the T-jct. Walk up this road (Sack Hill) and past the School of Infantry. About 200yds after the Roberts of Kandahar Road, turn R along a signposted path. This rises steeply to an old stile and turns R to skirt the R edge of a field. Cross a stile, turn R and bear L away from the fence towards the R edge of a hill fort (Battlesbury Hill). As the much-churned track goes L, turn R to go along the top of the outer wall of the fort. Follow this path round the fort including at one stage going over a stile. When you've turned 180° you meet a fence. Turn R to go over a stile. Now follow the R edge of the field downhill. At the bottom take the path ahead that runs between two fields. This leads to a metalled lane. Turn R and almost immediately bear L up the slope of Middle Hill.

(OSL 183/184: OSP 1220) (5.75m/9.25km)

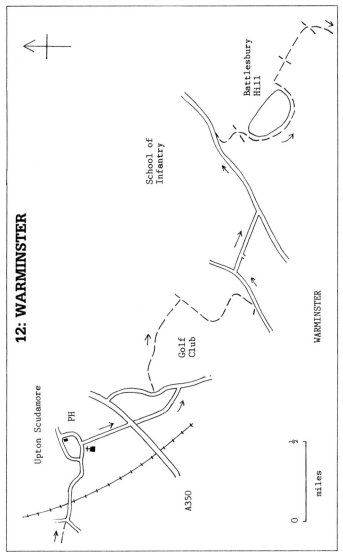

12: WARMINSTER

Upton Scudamore

PH

School of
Infantry

Battlesbury
Hill

Golf
Club

A350

WARMINSTER

0   miles

13: HEYTESBURY

The path follows the R edge of the field around the escarpment with views over Wylye Valley. Just after passing a small copse (R), bear R down the slope to a metalled lane. Go ahead for 20yds and turn R over a stile. Go up the hill to a second stile and on further up to the outside wall of another hill fort (Scratchbury Hill). Turn L and follow the path along the top of the wall. This eventually bends R with a fence close L. Walk on past an old stile to a stile in the fence. Go over this and bear R diagonally across the field to a solitary waymark post. Go straight over the X-track and continue roughly straight on with the fence close R. This continues past a gate. When the fence turns R, continue ahead towards a stile on the horizon. Continue over the next field and through a small wood. Carry straight on, downhill, with a fence close L to a minor road. Turn R to the A36(T). Bear slightly R to go down the road opposite into Heytesbury. When the main road bends R to The Angel, go straight on along a narrow lane. Before entering Mill Lane turn L, with tall conifers to R, to reach the River Wylye. Carry on with the river close R. The path follows the river to Mill Farm. Cross the footbridge and bear L to leave the mill buildings via a metal gate. Turn R along the lane and follow it as it loops over a stream. As the lane bends back R, take a stony path, that leads back across the stream. Go R over a stile and follow the hedge R for 250yds. Bear L across the field to the river (the right of way footbridge to L marked on OS map no longer exists) and turn R to cross a stile near a footbridge (L). Don't cross the river but turn R to go over another footbridge. Bear L to cross the field diagonally to another bridge. Continue on the same course to cross a stile and a further bridge into a hedged path. This passes over a broad farm track to continue along a narrower hedged path to a farm drive with a railway ahead. Turn L and walk along the dirt drive to a gate.

(OSL 184: OSP 1220) (4m/6.25km)

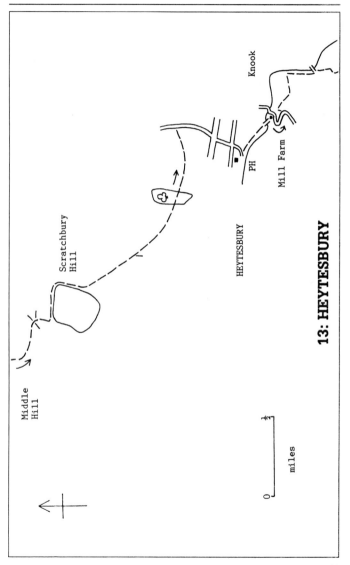

13: HEYTESBURY

14: UPTON LOVELL

Go through the gate and continue along the R edge of the field to cross a footbridge. The narrow path continues on to a driveway and then a road (turn L here for the Prince Leopold pub in Upton Lovell). Turn R and then L along the road. At a T-jct turn R. After 300yds this road bends R. Here turn L along a dirt track. The path now goes straight (although in various guises) for ³/₄ mile to a road. Turn R and follow the road which twists and turns, goes over the railway to reach Boyton. Turn L. The road bends sharp L and then, as it bends sharp R, go straight on over a stile. Turn L to follow the edge of the field to a brook and then turn R to walk along the L edge of some fields. After going over a stile, the field edge bends gently R and L. Now bear R towards a solitary post in the middle of the field and on across to a farm gate. Go through this, turn R and then shortly thereafter, L into Sherrington. Go past the church and, at a small junction, go R over a stream. When this lane turns R, go straight on. The clear grassy path goes under the railway with the River Wylye close L. When the river bends away, go straight on, over a stile. Follow the edge of this field for the next 600yds to a stile. Cross this and continue on to go over another stile. The path now passes some cottages to continue over a bridge. Turn R to go over a stile to a road. Turn R again and, after 50yds, L along a drive into Stockton Park.

(OSL 184: OSP 1220/1240) (4m/6.25km)

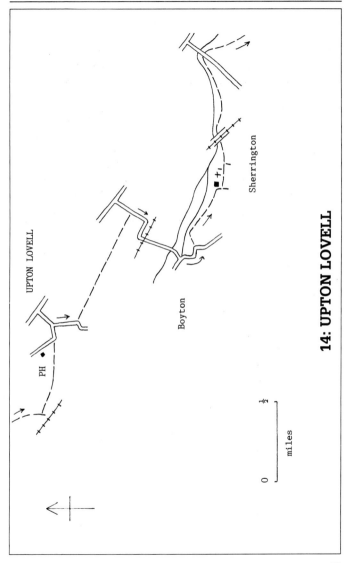

UPTON LOVELL

PH

Boyton

Sherrington

0   miles   ½

14: UPTON LOVELL

15 WYLYE

About 150yds after the drive has turned sharp R, go L through a kissing gate and follow the clear path ahead across parkland with Stockton Manor to L. Go through the kissing gate and turn L along the lane. Follow this past The Carriers pub and on for just over a mile until you pass the French château-like Bapton Manor. Turn L along a fenced path. Eventually this bends R to a gate. Follow the path round, over a gated footbridge and on to another gate and a footbridge over the river. At the lane, turn R. After passing the mill and the river, turn R through a gate to walk along the L bank of the river. The path leads under the dual carriageway of the A303 and over two stiles to reach a road. Turn R into the village of Wylye. Go past the Bell Inn and the Country Stores and bear R along Dyer Lane. Continue over Teapot Street to the end of the village. Turn L along a dirt drive which crosses the railway and continues into open country past a barn. Follow the bridleway round for $^3/_4$ mile to a point where the main drive ends near a chalk pit to the L. Don't take the more obvious path R but head in the direction of a gate about 150yds to L. Go through the gate and straight on to another. Continue up the next field to the head of the valley and through a gate. The path now goes up through another gate and out near some farm buildings R. Go straight on along a broad farm drive which soon bends R and then twists around some field edges to reach a broad X-track. Turn L and then L again at a T-jct along a concrete lane. After about $^2/_3$ mile, the lane bends L through beech trees. Just after the bend, turn R off the concrete lane along a wood path which skirts the R edge of the woodland. Cross the minor road and go up the path opposite.

(OSL 184: OSP 1240/1241) (6.25m/10km)

15: WYLYE

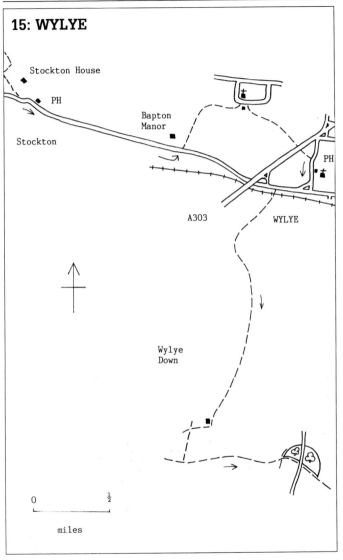

Stockton House

PH

Bapton
Manor

Stockton

A303

WYLYE

PH

Wylye
Down

0   ½

miles

16: OX DROVE

In just under ¹/₂ mile bear R (ie. don't go through the gate ahead) to continue through woodland along the Ox Drove. After 1¹/₂ miles, the path forks. Take the L-hand path which leads to some farm buildings with paths going L, half-L, half-R and a road going R. Take the half-R path uphill and along a dirt track. The drove continues over a cross track and on for another 1¹/₂ miles to a milestone (VI to Sarum). Bear L (ie. don't turn hard L along a signposted footpath) to go uphill, following the course of the power cables in the fields to the L.

(OSL 184: OSP 1241) (4m/6.25km)

Gateway, Sherrington - Section 14

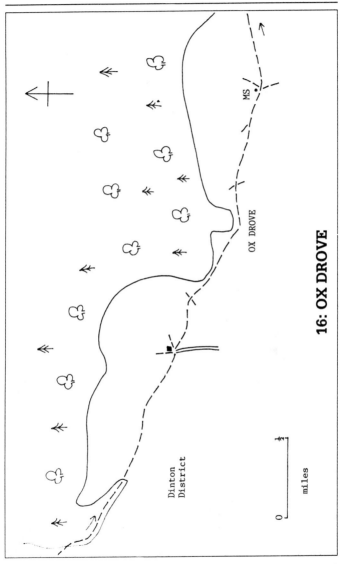

16: OX DROVE

17: WILTON

Continue along the drove for another 2 miles (you pass another milestone and go over a cross track) to reach some farm buildings. Here turn R and take the L-hand fork to descend to some houses on the outskirts of Wilton. Bear L to go behind some garages and downhill to a lane which goes past some bungalows. On reaching the main road, turn R under the railway and on to a T-jct near The Bell pub. Turn L and follow the road R. This road goes past the splendid Italianate church and into central Wilton with various shops and pubs. Go straight on at the crossroads in the direction of Wilton House. The road goes through a number of bends to reach a roundabout. Turn R along the A36 to the next set of traffic lights where (to much relief) we leave the main road. Turn L at the next junction into Quidhampton. This road passes The White Horse pub to reach a road fork. Turn R towards Lower Bemerton.

(OSL 184: OSP 1241) (4.25m/6.75km)

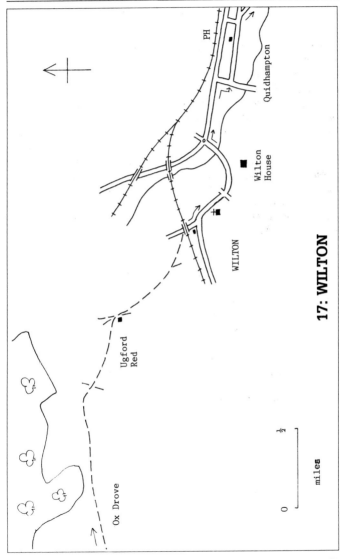

PH

Quidhampton

Wilton
House

WILTON

Ugford
Red

Ox Drove

17: WILTON

miles

$\frac{1}{2}$

0

18: SALISBURY

Follow the lane into Bemerton. Pass the parish church and a school to reach a small church (the Church of St Andrew) at a road junction. Go straight on here. Shortly after a small grocer's the road bends R and then L. As it straightens again, go R along a footpath which goes over a series of small streams of the River Nadder. Eventually, the path reaches a road at West Harnham. Turn L to go along the road for 600yds and then turn L to go along Town Path which goes past The Three Crowns and the Old Mill Hotel. This popular walk continues over meadows with views of Salisbury Cathedral R. On crossing the river, bear R to follow the road round to Beach's Bookshop and the centre of town. Turn R here if you wish to visit the cathedral. The walk continues L along the High Street and into the main shopping area. Just after W.H.Smith, turn R into New Canal. This leads to Milford Street which goes past the Red Lion Hotel, crosses Brown Street and on past the Trafalgar Hotel to a by-pass flyover. Keep straight on up Milford Hill to pass the youth hostel. At the Godolphin School bear R into Shadey Bower. This road bears L past St Martin's C of E School and over a railway. After going downhill, the road bends L. Turn R opposite Little Manor Nursing Home down Milford Mill Road. Cross the River Bourne and turn L along Queen Manor Road. Keep straight on along this road, ignoring two turnings L. This continues as a metalled lane into the Clarendon Park Estate. A $\frac{1}{4}$ mile after entering the estate, take the footpath R which leads diagonally across a field to a stile.

(OSL 184: OSP 1241/1262) (4.5m/7.25km)

18: SALISBURY

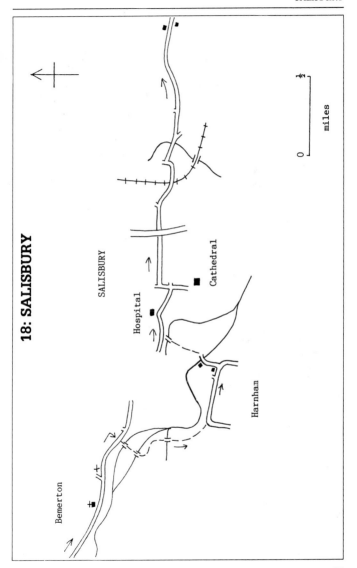

SALISBURY

Hospital

Cathedral

Bemerton

Harnham

miles

0

*Kings Somborne.
Section 22*

*Broughton dovecote.
Section 21*

Along the Clarendon Way

The Clarendon Way joins two of the nation's oldest cathedral cities, Salisbury and Winchester: twenty-five miles over the intervening low hills and the Test Valley. The walk, which takes coasters from Wiltshire into Hampshire, gains its name from the medieval palace which was once sited to the north-east of Salisbury. This spacious mansion which now exists only in the drawings of imaginative archaeologists was once a hunting lodge for the Norman kings. Henry II was the builder and Henry III converted a mere lodge into a palace. It was here, for example, that the Norman court spent its Christmas. By Henry VI's time, Clarendon was decidedly out of favour and the palace was sold to raise money. In the end, Charles II gave it away and by the eighteenth century it seems to have fallen into terminal disrepair.

After passing the palace, our way, meanwhile, continues through the pleasant village of Pitton to reach the Roman road at Middle Winterslow. The road was built as the direct route from Winchester to Old Sarum, the forerunner of Salisbury which is situated just a few miles north of the present city. We follow the road along its almost straight course for nearly 3 miles before veering north to Broughton. Here in the graveyard of the thirteenth century Norman church is a fine round dovecote, although at the time of my visits it seemed bereft of doves.

The Test is one of southern England's best trout rivers and beautiful too. Rising near the village of Ashe (near Overton), it runs via Whitchurch and Longparish to Stockbridge and Romsey and then on to the sea at Southampton. From the many bridges that cross the river, you can peer down into the spectacularly clear waters where the fine brown trout twist and turn seductively. The Test Way is a good walk of fifty miles from Totton (a point to the north-west of Southampton) to Inkpen Beacon. The only problem with the route is that after Longparish it doesn't follow the Test. Still, we can allow for some walker's licence as Inkpen is as good a spot to start or finish a long-distance walk as can be found.

Folly-baggers will enjoy Farley Mount, a peculiar pyramid shape building perched on a hill to the west of Winchester. The monument is typically British as it is dedicated not to some worthy person but to a horse. Indeed the said nag is reputed to be buried somewhere underneath. A plaque attempts to explain the rationale behind all this although frankly the view south is far more interesting. From Farley Mount, it is but a short stroll into the pleasant, if traffic plagued, city of Winchester. The cathedral is to the right of the shopping centre as we go through town. One of the little known facts about the place is that it is one of the longest cathedrals in Europe (at nearly 170 metres).

From the metropolis of Salisbury with its abundant supply of pubs, cafes and shops, it is only a short hop to Pitton and Middle Winterslow, both of which offer a small shop and a pub (Silver Plough, Pitton is GPG). The next opportunity for such service is in Broughton and then Kings Somborne. There now follows a facility free 8-9 mile walk into the centre of Winchester. The old city has a wide range of facilities including no fewer than four CAMRA recommended pubs: County Arms, Exchange, Fulflood Arms and King Alfred, and three GPG pubs: Wykeham Arms, Eclipse and Queen, as well as the Bell, Abbey, Black Boy, Roebuck and Royal Oak.

Farley Mount.
Section 23

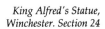

King Alfred's Statue,
Winchester. Section 24

19: PITTON

The footpath leads diagonally over the field to cross a stile. Turn R along the chalky, farm track which winds its way up the hill. After passing King Manor Cottage (L), turn L along a broad dirt road. To L here are the remains of Clarendon Palace, a Norman hunting lodge that gives its name to the Clarendon Way. After 300yds, a gap in the trees L gives a view of a field. One hundred yards after this, take a minor path that leaves the main track L. This path passes through a variety of different types of forestry including oak woodland, new conifer plantation and mature conifer. Keep a roughly straight course throughout for just over a mile before coming to an open field L and then descending to Four Cottages and some farm buildings. Take a path to the L of the cottages that goes behind them. This follows the edge of a wood and copse with a fence close L. Within ¼ mile the path becomes fenced, then hedged, before winding around Pitton Primary School and coming out over a stile to a road. Turn R and then L along Pitton High Street. After passing the post office/general store, turn R along a path near a bus stop and opposite the parish church. The route goes up through a small play area to a road. Turn L. Just before the end of this road bear R up a bridleway which starts to the L of a garage. This well-defined path goes up the hill with fine views L. Before reaching the top take the fenced path L that stays close to the edge of the escarpment. After a short distance the fence on the L disappears and we follow the fence R in the direction of the church on the skyline ahead. This path crosses a stile and takes a line along the L edge of a field. When the fence turns L keep straight on.

(OSL 184: OSP 1262/1241/1242) (4.25m/6.75km)

19: PITTON

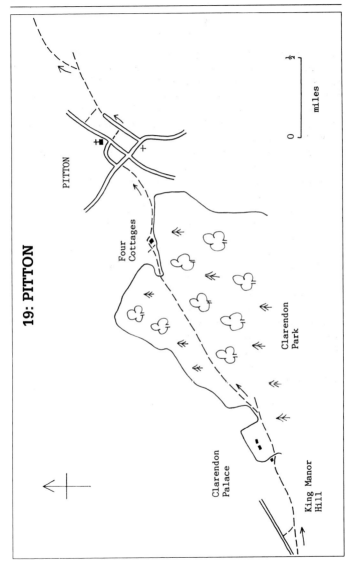

PITTON

Four
Cottages

Clarendon
Park

Clarendon
Palace

King Manor
Hill

0   ½

miles

20: WINTERSLOWS

Keep straight on towards some farm buildings. The path leads to an alley between some houses and then out to a road. Go straight across the road to take a path to the R of All Saints Church. Cross the stile and follow the hedge L around to another stile. Turn R to reach a further stile. Do not cross here but turn L to walk along a fenced path that leads L and then R into a wood. The route now meanders through woodland to a point where it goes downhill and turns L. Here keep an eye open to R for the much clearer path that goes up the hill in a north-easterly direction. This leads to a dirt drive (Cobb Lane) with a house to L. When you reach the metalled Roman Road, keep straight on past The Flood and out to Middleton Road. Turn L to go downhill. At the bottom, as the main road turns R, carry straight on along the minor lane called The Causeway. This passes some houses and deteriorates into a dirt road before bending R. Here go L into a playing field. Cross the stile and follow some power cables up the hill to a gate. Bear L and then R to go along Red Lane. This arrives at the main road (Cunville Hill) near a telephone box. Walk on for about 150yds and turn L along Mill Lane. Within 20yds, turn R along a dirt track known as Easton Common Hill. This Roman road now descends with fine views L. Go straight over the crossroads at Little Buckholt Farm and up a metalled lane. This rises sharply to Buckholt Farm. Here as the road turns R, carry straight on with the main farm buildings to L. The way bends gradually L to reach a green road. Turn R to go down the hill.

(OSL 184: OSP 1242) (4.25m/6.75km)

20: WINTERSLOW

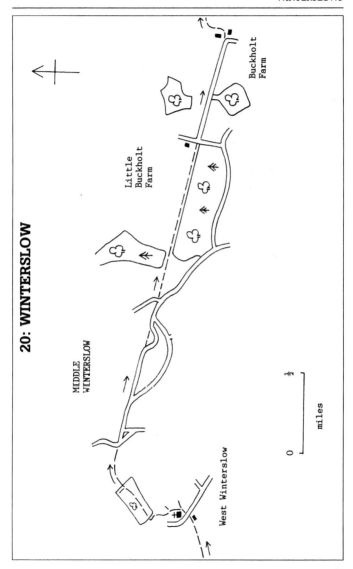

MIDDLE
WINTERSLOW

Little
Buckholt
Farm

Buckholt
Farm

West Winterslow

0   ½

miles

21: BROUGHTON

Where the route forks, take the R-hand track for $^1/_2$ mile to a green lane crossroads. Go straight on for another $^1/_2$ mile to join a wider green lane that is splendidly bordered with mature beech trees. Turn L here to go downhill through a patch of yew woodland. This leads to a metalled drive. Follow this L for 600yds into Broughton and the Salisbury Road. Bear R and then L along Queenwood Road. Continue to a T-jct near the Greyhound pub. If you wish, you may turn R here to see St Mary's Church, visit the Tally Ho pub or stock up on provisions in the small general store. If not bear L and then R to go down Rectory Lane. This goes over Wallop Brook and down a narrow hedged path to the L of Waterside. Cross a stile and turn R. Continue along this edge of the field for about $^2/_3$ mile to enter a green lane. Turn R and then, after about 10yds, L to walk up the hill and to the left of a small stand of trees (Hayter's Copse). This path now continues in the same general direction for a further $1^1/_2$ miles before coming out to a road.

(OSL 185: OSP 1242) (4m/6.5km)

21: BROUGHTON

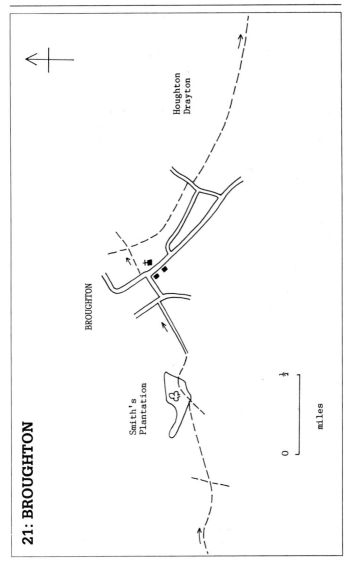

BROUGHTON

Houghton
Drayton

Smith's
Plantation

0    $\frac{1}{2}$

miles

22: KINGS SOMBORNE

At the road turn L. Walk for about 250yds and, just before a bungalow, turn R down a private road. This leads to a bridge over the River Test and on to a farm drive which winds its way past Blacklake Farm. After two more river bridges, the drive passes via a gate onto an old railway line that marks the course of the Test Way (and before that the Andover Canal). Go straight on, up the hill to a metalled lane. Continue straight on with views to Kings Somborne in the valley to the R. Immediately before reaching a road, turn R down a footpath which follows the L-hand edge of a field.This goes downhill to the bottom L-hand corner where there is a stile. Cross this into the road (Cowdrove Hill) and turn R to reach Stockbridge Road (A3057). Turn R and then almost immediately L to go along Old Vicarage Road. Follow the course of the dried up brook R and cross it near a Spa grocer. Continue on to pass the Andover Arms. After about ¹/₄ mile, pass the thatched Red Hill Cottage on the R and turn R up a farm track. This rises up a hill along the L-hand edge of a field into another field. The path now descends into a third field. Keeping the hedge close L, cross three sets of paired stiles before bearing L to the far corner of the field. Cross the stile into some thin woodland and continue out to a more prominent track which marks the course of a Roman road. Bear L to follow the straight course of the old road. At a green lane crossroads, ignore the bridleway sign pointing R and continue straight on. The lane eventually bears R down a track lined with yew trees out to a field. Continue downhill into a quiet and remote valley. At the bottom, the route turns 90° L to follow a yew hedge out to a road.

(OSL 185: OSP 1242/1263) (4.5m/7.25km)

The Old Mill, Harnham

The River Itchen near Ovington
House at Selborne

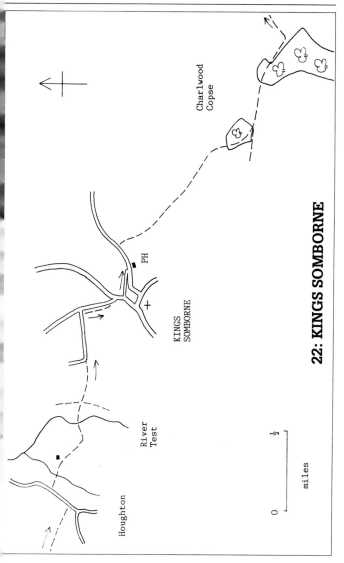

22: KINGS SOMBORNE

Charlwood Copse

PH

KINGS SOMBORNE

River Test

Houghton

0   ½   miles

23: FARLEY MOUNT

Turn 90° R to go up a grassy path that separates two fields. This leads to a fenced path which goes up the hill to some more yew trees and then skirts around the edge of the wood with good views L. At the top of the hill, the wood ends and we enter Farley Mount Country Park. Go straight on along the broad path (deviating briefly to get a closer look at Farley Mount monument R) to reach a car park and then a minor road. Bear L of the Country Park notice to take a path that bears away from the road and into some open birch woodland. As this path bends R, take another that goes into some beech woodland L. This indistinct route goes through the wood, following a line that bears slightly R. At a forest road, turn L. The road then almost immediately bends R to pass two car parks. Go past the barrier and follow the open track R. Ignore a clear path through the wood L. Instead continue on for a further 20yds to turn L into an open area with forest L and a slope to the road R. Keep to the L-hand edge of this popular open area and along an obvious track that goes through the thicket ahead. This goes uphill slightly and then meets a green lane. Turn R to reach a road and then L to walk along it. After 200yds (and just after an entrance to West Wood), take a path L into the wood. Ignore clear tracks R until you reach another entrance to West Wood L. Turn R here and then R again to pass down a narrow dirt lane (a Forestry Authority permissive trail), the entrance of which is festooned with waymark notices of all descriptions. This pathway continues for $1/2$ mile to reach a gate. Cross the road to the entrance of Crabwood Nature Reserve. Turn R to follow a clear fenced path. Walk on with the fence of the reserve close L to reach another road near a house. Turn L. This metalled road (Lanham Lane) goes past Crabwood Farm and then some more houses before deteriorating into a dirt track.

(OSL 185: OSP 1263/1264) (4m/6.5km)

23: FARLEY MOUNT

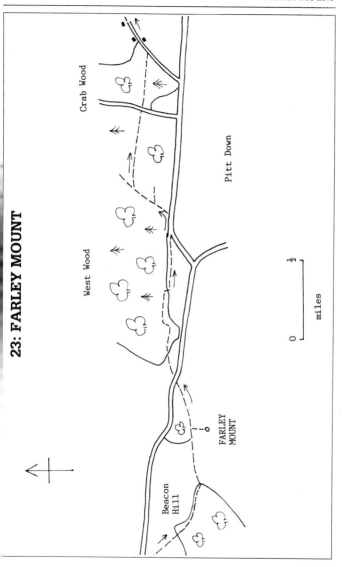

Crab Wood

West Wood

Pitt Down

Beacon Hill

FARLEY MOUNT

0   ½

miles

24: WINCHESTER

The dirt track gradually bends R to pass a collection of communication aerials R. Ultimately the track meets a metalled lane. Bear L, past a scout's campsite, to go down and then up a hill with a golf course L. At the top of the hill, turn L (leaving the Clarendon Way) along Sarum Road. This road passes the golf club L and a school R before going on to a pavement neatly shielded from a road by a hedge. After $1/2$ mile, continue straight on at a crossroads and then out to meet Romsey Road. Here turn L. This road now goes straight into the centre of Winchester, passing the hospital and through West Gate. The BR station is signposted L along this road. Pass through the pedestrianised shopping streets to walk past the bus station to King Alfred's statue. (Turn R off the High Street to see the Cathedral.) Walk on, with the statue to L, into Broadway. Go over a bridge next to the National Trust's Winchester City Mill and turn L, just before the Cricketer's pub, into Water Lane. This road runs between the River Itchen on the L and some houses R. At a road bridge bear R along Wales Lane to pass The Ship Inn and the First In - Last Out and then into the Winnall Industrial Estate. Just after Nickel Close, turn L along a narrow lane with bungalows to the R. After 200yds, cross the stile into a narrow field.

(OSL 185: OSP 1264/1243) (4m/6.5km)

24: WINCHESTER

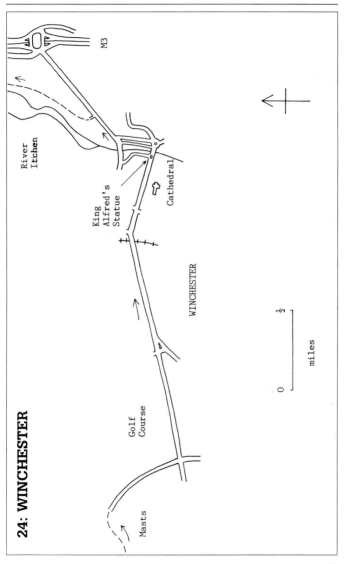

M3

River
Itchen

King
Alfred's
Statue

Cathedral

WINCHESTER

Golf
Course

Masts

0   ½

miles

25: ITCHEN ABBAS

Walk with hedge L to a stile and a path which after $^{1}/_{4}$ mile meets the Itchen and turns R under two bridges. After the second, go L to stay near the river until you reach a green lane. Keep the same basic course with Easton Down and the M3 R. Keep to L side of the next field to a tennis court. Turn L to go past a house and over the Itchen. Walk along a causeway and then bear R over a stile to follow a track across pasture to a bridge over another Itchen tributory. After a few yards on a road, turn R through a kissing gate. Cross the field (with river R) to a stile in the top L corner and repeat this for the next, larger, field. Cross a stile and turn R along a road for 50yds before turning R over a stile. Follow the R edge of this field to a gate and a tunnel under the M3. Follow the path L over a stile and turn R. Walk with fence R to a stile into another field to continue now with fence L. Cross a minor road to take the path to R of a house into a field. Keep close to the fence R. After a stile, go straight to follow the path past gardens to a lane. Turn L and, opposite St Swithun's church, go R past the village hall to a kissing gate. Continue on the same line across a field. At a gate and fence walk with fence L to a kissing gate. Follow the L edge of this field then cross a stile to follow the R edge of the next. In the far R corner, a stile leads to a fenced path and a lane. Bear L and almost immediately R along a fenced path. After a stile, keep the same course across fields with the Itchen R. After a kissing gate, a sign offers two routes either side of a paddock. Take the R-hand route, ie. with fence L. This goes through a series of gates to a X-track. Go straight on eventually to reach houses R and then a road at Itchen Abbas. (Plough Inn is a short walk L.) Turn R along the road, over two bridges and past Avington Park. As the road bends R, turn L and then R up a farm track. After 300yds, the route turns L. Walk on for $^{1}/_{3}$ mile.

(OSL 185: OSP 1243) (5m/8km)

25: ITCHEN ABBAS

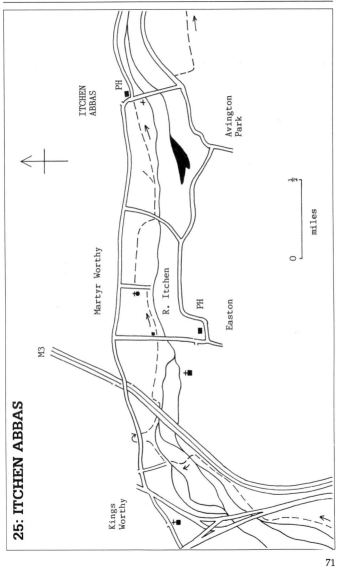

Through the Leafy Hampshire Lanes

There's some splendid walking country in Hampshire. The gentle rolling hills are covered in rich, productive farm land and speckled with pleasant St Mary Mead-like villages. There's many a delightful trout stream, numerous fine pubs and an abundance of wildlife. It's all curiously unspoilt given the increasing push for those "executive" housing projects that plague such vacant sites within commuting distance of London. However you can't help but feel that you have to see the place now before it gets trampled all over in the name of development. Best do it soon.

The route of the Southern Coast to Coast east of Winchester starts by going along the Itchen Way, a long-distance path of twenty-seven miles that begins by the Solent in Southampton and ends near the village of Hinton Ampner to the south of New Alresford. The River Itchen is another one of Hampshire's fine sprawling waterways whose crystal clear waters are such a delight. We follow it through Itchen Abbas and Itchen Stoke and on to the watercress beds of New Alresford. Here, as all steam buffs will know, is the wonderful Watercress Line - otherwise known as the Mid-Hants Railway - which runs from Alresford to Alton. Broad Street has some fine colour-washed Georgian houses and a range of curiously old-fashioned shops. Long-distance path collectors will also note that the village plays host to the seventy-mile-long Wayfarer's Walk that connects Inkpen Beacon with the harbour at Emsworth near Portsmouth.

The Southern Coast to Coast meanwhile goes east through Bighton and on to Selborne. Even without Gilbert White people would come to Selborne. This is one of those places that abounds with good Sunday afternoon strolls which the Selborne Hangar and surrounding National Trust lands are more than happy to provide. The Reverend Gilbert White however adds to the attraction. White was one of the nation's first naturalists and his book describing the local flora and fauna is a classic. His house is open to the public and there are exhibits both on the local hero as well as the more universal hero of Captain Oates (he who went outside for some time during Scott's attempt on the south pole).

At Ludshott Common, close to the Surrey border, are the Waggoners (formerly the Wakeners) Wells: a series of man-made ponds which are said to be a source of the River Wey. The valley in which they sit, known as Hammer Bottom, was once home to a number of ironworks and the Wells were probably built as header ponds for an ironworking mill further downstream. Whatever their origin, they make a pleasant spot at which to leave the fine county of Hampshire.

There is a small selection of pubs between Winchester and Alresford, for example The Plough Inn is at Itchen Abbas and the Bush Inn (GPG) is at Ovington. Alresford itself has a useful range of shops and several pubs. The Horse & Groom is GPG. You won't find any more shops between Alresford and Selborne but the pub at Bighton, the Three Horseshoes, is CAMRA & GPG. Selborne itself has a couple of pubs, the Selborne Arms (GPG) and the Queen's Hotel, and a small local store. There is also at least one cafe. The Red Lion at Oakhanger is CAMRA & GPG but after that there is nothing until Grayshott. Here, after appearing into civilisation from the Waggoners Wells, there is a row of shops and The Fox & Pelican pub.

The Devil's Punchbowl, Hindhead. Section 32

*Selborne Church.
Section 29*

*Sundial Clock on
Thursley Church.
Section 32*

26: ALRESFORD

The path passes through a small copse and then out to a field. At a fence turn L downhill to cross a stile in the fence R. Descend to another stile into a road. Turn R to pass Yavington Farm. As the road bends R and starts to climb, bear L following a path sign along the drive of Yavington Mead and then past the french windows of the house to a stile. Go straight on across the field to a double set of stiles into another field. Keep to the L side to cross a stile in the top L corner. Turn L along a path which leads to two bridges over the Itchen. After the second, go straight on across the field, over a farm bridge and, bearing R, out to a gate. Two stiles take you into a driveway and on to a road. Turn R. After passing a bus stop, turn R down Water Lane (signposted to Ovington). This lane reaches a bridge and goes alongside and then over the Itchen before reaching the Bush Inn, Ovington. Turn L along a lane with a stream R. Keep on this quiet lane until you reach the main Alresford-Winchester road (A31). Cross the road and walk up a signposted slope opposite, over an embankment and on through scrub to a hedged path. At the bottom of the slope, cross the road and walk on up a road to a ford. After crossing a bridge, go straight on along a narrow lane which winds between watercress beds to a road (Spring Gardens). Go straight on to a road near the Cricketers pub. Turn L to walk along the pavement for $^3/_4$ mile into Alresford. Turn R into West Street where there are numerous shops and pubs. Pass the Bell Hotel and the Swan Hotel and turn L down the L-side of Broad St. Walk on to Mill Hill which descends to pass Tower Mill and continues with a stream R. This soon reaches watercress beds and then a road. Turn R and R again to walk along the B3046 for about 50yds. Turn L along a road signposted to Bighton. Walk on for $^1/_2$ mile with watercress to R. When the road bends L, cross the stile R and continue along the R edge of the field.

(OSL 185: OSP 1243) (5.25m/8.5km)

26: ALRESFORD

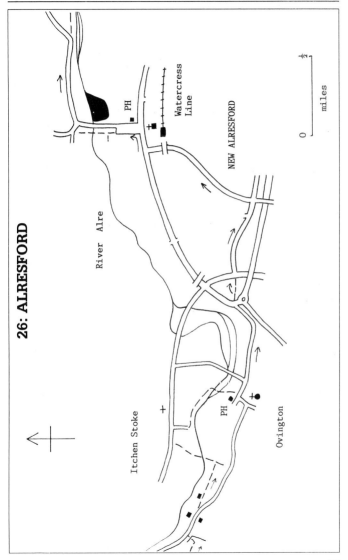

River Alre

PH

Watercress Line

NEW ALRESFORD

Itchen Stoke

PH

Ovington

0   miles   ½

27: BIGHTON

This path leads to a gate and a green lane. Cross the stile opposite into a field and continue along the same course with the hedge close L. At the end of this field, bear R to a stile. Cross this and turn L and then R to go along a hedged green lane. The lane eventually passes the Malt House and the farm yard of Manor Farm. When you reach a road, bear L and then R to follow the road signposted to Medstead and Wield. The road passes the Three Horseshoes and carries on to a turning R signposted to Ropley. Follow this quiet road (Bighton Dean Road) to a junction. Bear L, now following signs to North Street. By a red brick house (Takuma), the road bends 90° R. We, however, keep straight on along a green lane for about 300yds. Just before the lane opens out slightly, there is a hidden turning R. If you reach a point where the lane broadens, you've gone too far. The track is Gullet Lane and should now be followed for 1^1/$_3$ miles. After passing over a green lane crossroads and through the edge of a wood, the path descends to a railway embankment. Turn R here to go through the tunnel and continue R to reach the A31 (Four Marks is to L). Cross the dual carriageway to a footpath sign and a stile. Take the path which goes straight up the hill and bear L at the top to reach a metalled lane.

(OSL 185: OSP 1244) (4.5m/7.25km)

27: BIGHTON

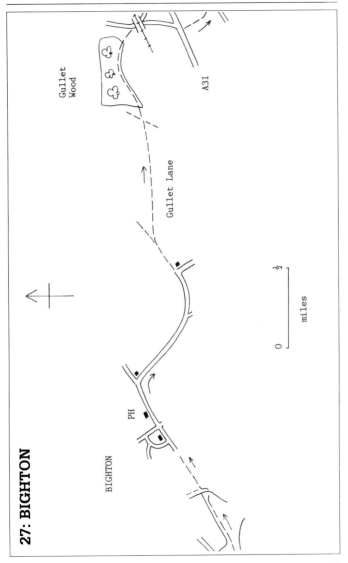

BIGHTON

PH

Gullet
Wood

Gullet Lane

A31

0 ½ miles

28: KITWOOD

A footpath sign just across the metalled lane points along a hedged path into Old Down Wood. Keep to the broad dirt drive, ignoring a path sign R. When you reach a X-track, go straight on and follow the ever narrowing path through the wood to come out eventually on a road near a thatched cottage. Cross the road to mount a small embankment into a field. Turn L to follow the edge of this field to a power line post and then bear R across the field to a stile marked by a yellow arrow. The path now goes via another stile into a hedged pathway with a pond L. At the end, cross the stile and bear R up some steps. This leads to the drive of a large house (R). Take a line that goes to the L of a wooden lodge and out to a stile. Keep to L edge of the field and cross the stile at the end. Turn R along a lane and, after 10yds, turn L to go along a by-way that follows the L edge of a massive field for about a mile to reach a road. Go directly across the road and then up a green lane to skirt some woodland. As the woods end, the lane turns R to Newtonwood Farm. Just after the house, turn L to go along a metalled drive and past some barns. Continue straight on over a gate into a fenced path that leads to another gate into a field. Follow the R edge of the field with a woodland R and a valley L. Continue to the top R corner of the field where a stile leads to a farm drive. This descends to another drive. Turn L to reach a road by an old toll house. Cross the road and go straight up the hill to a gap in the hedge that is surrounded by a gaggle of yellow posts. Follow the signs R to a point where you go down some steps to cross an old railway line. Climb the steps on the other side and turn L. When you reach a gully and some steps made of old railway sleepers, turn R to resume the path (yellow arrows point the way). The trail now winds through the woods and out to a field. Head towards a yellow square high on a tree on the opposite side of the field.

(OSL 186: OSP 1244) (4.25m/6.75km)

28: KITWOOD

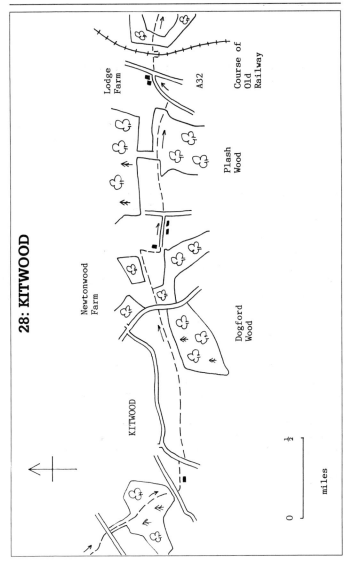

Lodge Farm

A32

Course of Old Railway

Plash Wood

Newtonwood Farm

Dogford Wood

KITWOOD

0   ½   miles

29: SELBORNE

Go through a narrow length of wood and out to go R of a pylon to
a stile and on to another stile in the hedge just R of a house. Take the
private drive past the house and a tennis court to a gate and stile.
Bear L across the field to a gap in the fence to a road. Turn R and walk
through Newton Valence. Just after the war memorial (L) turn L
along a bridleway. This bears L and then bends R along a track. Near
a gate, the path bends L to a stile. Do not cross but turn R along a
bridleway to Selborne Common. Just beyond the NT notice, go
straight on along a broad path through open woods for $^2/_3$ mile. On
reaching a row of houses R, bear L to a stone and a view down to
Selborne. Descend the steps L. At the bottom go through a kissing
gate and follow the path to a car park. Continue to a minor road and
bear L to the B3006. Turn L to pass the Selbourne Arms, a small shop
and the Gilbert White Museum. Just before the Selbourne Gallery,
turn R into St Mary's Parish Church churchyard by the R-hand gate.
Go through the graveyard to enter Church Meadow. Go down the
hill towards the brick built hut, through a gate and turn L along a
metalled lane. Pass a house and follow the woodland track to a gate
and stile. Cross into the field and continue with a hedge close R. Go
through two gates, passing a bungalow, to a metalled lane which
comes in R. Before entering Priory Farm, cross a stile L and then a
small footbridge. Go up the hill to another stile in the corner of the
field. Cross the green lane and a stile into a field. Walk straight
across, under some cables to a concrete footbridge over a brook
which runs along the bottom of the valley. Bear L and walk along an
indistinct path with the brook L to a stile in a row of trees with a
small bridge just beyond. Cross the next stile in a hedge. Keep this
course to cross a stile in the corner of the field and on to a further
stile. keep the fence close L to reach a 5-way footpath sign.

(OSL 186: OSP 1244) (4.5m/7.25km)

29: SELBORNE

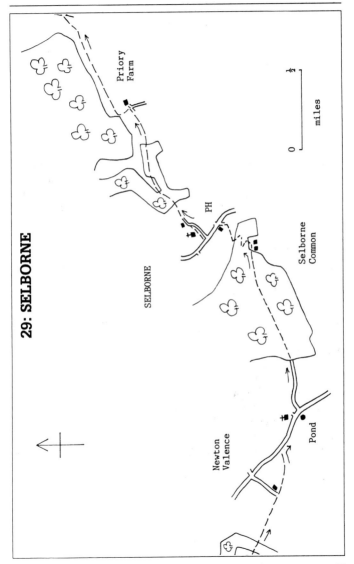

Priory
Farm

PH

SELBORNE

Selborne
Common

Newton
Valence

Pond

0 — ½ miles

30: BROXHEAD COMMON

Bear R to cross a stile. Turn L along a track towards Chapel Farm. Keep the farmhouse L to reach a road. Turn L for $1/2$ mile (passing The Red Lion). Just after a telephone box, turn R past the village hall to a footpath sign. Bear L through open woods onto Shortheath Common. Continue under power lines and to L of a house with a corrugated iron fence. The track bears R to meet a X-track. Ten yards on, bear L onto a less obvious path that goes L of bungalows. Continue over a wide X-track to a small path that winds between bushes to a stile. Cross two fields to go over a stile onto a railway embankment. Bear L and go down into the next field. Maintain the same course through a gap in the far hedge to cross a small bridge over a brook (with bedstead gates). Go through the narrow orchard to cross a drive and enter a gap in the hedge. Cross the stile and turn R. This leads via a further stile to a golf course. Bear L and walk on with a fence close R to a stile and a lane. Turn R at the T-jct and R again at the next T-jct. Follow this lane for a mile to reach the Petersfield Road. Turn L and cross the road to a lay-by at Broxhead Common. Turn R past the Ministry of Defence notice (NB. access may very occasionally be prohibited). Bear L to take a track that rises for 250yds to a wire fence. Bear R with fence close L to a road. Cross this and turn L to a lay-by. Go R into a nature reserve and bear L along a broad path to a fenced path. At the end, bear R with a wood L. At the bottom of the hill turn R with woods L. The path bends L uphill. Just before a gate, turn R through a gate and along a fenced path. Go through a gate and descend steeply to cross the River Wey into a wood. At the end of the wood turn L to a gate then R uphill with hedge R and fence L. Eventually the path turns L to a road. Turn L and L again into Curtis Lane. Almost immediately, turn R over a stile to cross the field diagonally. Go over four stiles to a road.

(OSL 186: OSP 1244/1245) (5.75m/9.25km)

30: BROXHEAD COMMON

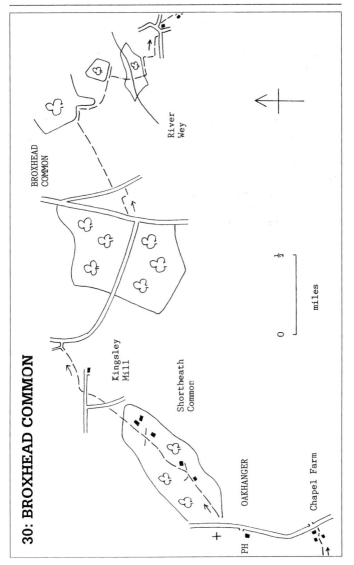

BROXHEAD COMMON

River Wey

Kingsley Mill

Shortheath Common

OAKHANGER

Chapel Farm

PH

0   ½   miles

31: LUDSHOTT COMMON

Walk to the end and turn R around the edge of a school field to a road. Go straight on to another road. Turn L and then R into Longcross Hill. At the bottom, when the road bends L, go straight on a path to R of a house. Cross a lane and along another path to a road. Turn L and then R down Bowcott Hill. This crosses a stream and goes uphill. At the top, bear R to walk along Headley Hill Road for $1/2$ mile. When the road turns L go straight along a dirt path into a conifer wood. The path bends R and descends to a road. Continue to a road junction and turn L along Pond Road. After passing Thorndene, go straight on along a forest path into Gentles Copse. This goes through trees to a point where there are two path junctions. At the first bear R and at the second bear L with the end result of going straight on onto Ludshott Common. Continue with woods R and slope L. After a $1/3$ mile, another starburst of paths can cause confusion. Paths go L, far L, R and straight on. Take the R-hand turn uphill with woods R. This crosses a major path near a seat and carries on to go down and then up another path. Go straight on to pass a house L to a gate. Cross the field with a fence L to a stile. Descend into woodland to a further stile and turn R along a path downhill to a footbridge. Don't cross the bridge but walk with the stream R. Shortly the stream broadens to the first of the Waggoners Wells. Two more are passed before the path reaches a road with a ford R. Don't cross but take the bridleway with stream to R. This passes some smaller wells. Cross at the dam of one of them to walk on along the R bank through woodland to a dirt road. Take the second signposted bridleway L up a hill to a drive. Turn L to reach Headley Road, Grayshott (turn R for shops and pub). Cross the road and go up Whitmore Vale Road to the R of the Church of St Luke. Within a few yards, turn R along Church Lane. At the end, turn L to go down a slope.

(OSL 186: OSP 1245) (5m/8km)

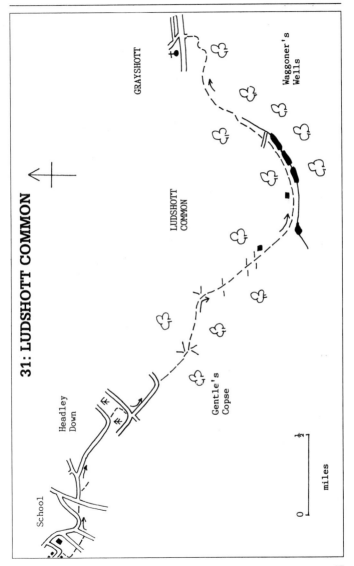

31: LUDSHOTT COMMON

GRAYSHOTT

Waggoner's
Wells

LUDSHOTT
COMMON

Headley
Down

Gentle's
Copse

School

miles

0   ½

31A: HASLEMERE TO HINDHEAD

This section does not form part of the Southern Coast to Coast but is the western most end of the Greensand Way. Only those walkers who wish to complete the entire GW should follow the route described on this page.

The Greensand Way starts at the Old Town Hall in Haslemere High Street. Walk down the High Street on the L-hand pavement to pass the war memorial, Rumpole's Coaching Inn and then the Georgian Hotel. As you pass the latter, keep an eye open for a narrow alleyway L. Take this narrow path between some houses and then out to reach Church Lane. Turn L and cross the road to go over the railway and along High Lane with St Bartholomew's Church on the opposite side of the street. The road bends R to cross Weycombe Road and then Kiln Fields. Continue up the road for about 150yds to a path which leaves on the L-hand side of the road opposite Ventnor. Take the alleyway to the R of the entrance to Lanreath. At a road, cross to a stile and then along a path with houses L and fields R. This leads out to a lane. Turn L and then R. Just before a building take the L-hand fork which starts as a metalled lane but deteriorates into a woodland path. At another minor road, turn R to pass some fine houses. After about $1/4$ mile, the L-hand side is thick woodland. After passing a postbox and almost opposite the entrance to Little Scotstoun, a footpath leaves the road and bears L into the trees. This clear path takes a relatively straight course out to an area of gorse and bracken with a fine view to L. Soon the path descends to cross another path and then goes uphill. When the path forks, take the L-hand track. As you pass a house called Sheiling, the main path bends R, take a less obvious L fork. With houses L, the path soon arrives at Hindhead near the Devil's Punch Bowl Hotel.

(OSL 186: OSP 1245) (2.75m/4.5km)

31A: HASLEMERE TO HINDHEAD

HINDHEAD

PH

Little Scotstoun

BR

Old
Town
Hall

HASLEMERE

0   ½

miles

32: HINDHEAD

Near the bottom of the valley, turn R to walk through woodland with houses R. This path eventually reaches a metalled lane. Turn R. At the road turn L and then L again along the A3. Carry straight on at traffic lights to reach the Devil's Punch Bowl Hotel. Just after the hotel bear R at the Hindhead Common notice. This wide track takes a relatively straight course, bearing away from the A3. After $^1/_3$ mile, the path passes a seat and promises to bend R. Before it does, turn L uphill. Go through the car park to a trig point. Turn L to pass Gibbet Hill Cross to a barrier. Turn L for a short distance and then R along a dirt road (the old Portsmouth Road) for $^2/_3$ mile. When the track meets the A3, cross and bear R along the path opposite. Follow this meandering track, ignoring all turn offs, for about a mile to a road. Turn R to walk for $^1/_4$ mile until the road bends R. Shortly after Hedge Farm, turn L up the drive to a narrow path between a hedge and a fence. This winds around the garden of the farm to a stile. The path now follows the L edge of a series of fields and crosses three stiles. At the end of the furthest field, the line is forced R along a dirt lane. This joins another dirt lane and continues downhill. After 150yds, turn R opposite Smallbrook. Cross the stile and head towards the top R corner of the field to another stile. This goes into a fenced path and crosses three stiles to enter Thursley church yard. Bear R with church L to a stepped stile. (Before leaving check your watch with the church clock!) Turn L to walk down the lane. As the road bends L, go straight on along a track to reach a house at a dead end. Go through the metal gate and bear diagonally R across the field to another gate. This leads to a path which in turn leads to the A3. Cross the dual carriageway and walk up the metalled drive signposted to Cosford Farm. The driveway bends R at one point to reveal views of Cosford House to L.

(OSL 186: OSP 1245) (5.5m/8.75km)

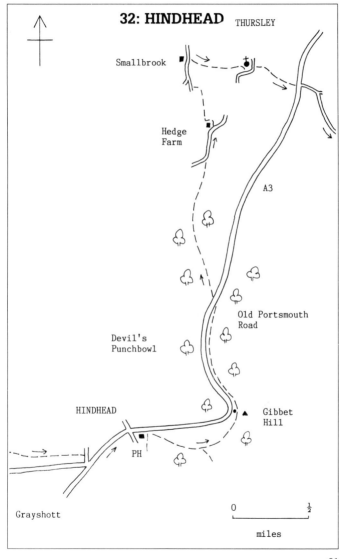

32: HINDHEAD

THURSLEY

Smallbrook

Hedge
Farm

A3

Old Portsmouth
Road

Devil's
Punchbowl

HINDHEAD

Gibbet
Hill

PH

Grayshott

0          $\frac{1}{2}$

miles

On the Greensand Ridge

The Greensand Way runs for 105 miles across the hills of Surrey and the fruit fields of Kent: from Haslemere in the west to a rather non-descript end point to the north-east of Hamstreet. It's a fine walk that has been sadly upstaged by its older, more illustrious neighbours: the North Downs Way and the South Downs Way. Such neglect is unworthy. The hills to the south of the A25 are every bit as good as those to the north and each is blessed with a fine view over the Surrey plain or the Kentish Weald.

The Greensand Way was originally devised by Geoffrey Hollis and other local ramblers. It was opened in a series of distinct phases. The fifty-five mile Surrey section was opened and waymarked in 1982 from Haslemere via Hindhead, Holmbury St Mary, Leith Hill, Dorking, Reigate Heath to Limpsfield. The thirty-mile West Kent section followed in April 1986. This joined the Surrey section at Limpsfield Chart and ran via Chartwell. Toy's Hill, Ide Hill, Sevenoaks Weald and West Peckham to Yalding. The final stretch, the twenty mile East Kent section, was opened in April 1989 and runs south of Maidstone and west of Ashford to finish near Hamstreet.

The Greensand ridge along which the route passes is an outcrop of sedimentary sandstones that stretches all the way along the northern side of the central Weald. Although predominantly yellow, the mineral glauconite occasionally gives the stone a greenish tinge - hence the name "greensand". These sandstones were laid down when the entire area was covered by sea; some 10,000,000 to 20,000,000 years ago. The layers of chalk that form the North and South Downs are even younger and were deposited on top of our sands. After these times of deposition, there followed a period of compression when the whole area of the Weald was lifted and contorted. The chalk and greensand layers in what would have been the Weald mountains were then eroded away. Today, in the central Weald, no layers of chalk or greensand remain. The low, flat Weald consists primarily of what are known as Wealden clays and sands.

Only the outer chalk and greensand layers prevail as the present day North and South Downs and as the Greensand Ridge along which the Southern Coast to Coast takes its course.

The sandy soils of the greensand ridge are fast draining and tend to lose any nutrients that they may contain. Thus across the hills of Surrey and, to a lesser extent, west Kent, the predominant vegetation is either heathland or planted conifer woods. Such heath is now a scarce commodity in England and Wales. It is a unique habitat that in the past has not been viewed sympathetically by planners and developers. In more recent years the conservation bodies, such as the Royal Society for Protection of Birds, have campaigned for its protection pointing out that this could be the last chance for many of our rarest animals such as the sand lizard and the Dartford warbler. Now, hopefully, we may actually be able to save what remains. It's a close run thing and even in the areas that are left, the shear numbers of visitors may still exert severe pressure on the remaining wildlife. Further east, the greensand ridge gradually subsides and the country from Sevenoaks to Pluckley is much lusher. Here the nutrient rich soils of the Garden of England predominate to play host to the fruit growing areas of central Kent. By the time the Greensand Way reaches Great Chart, the ridge has all but gone and it plays no further part in determining the lie of the land around us.

The Southern Coast to Coast follows the Greensand Way from Hindhead to its end point near Hamstreet. The only section excluded from the route is that between Haslemere and Hindhead; a distance of just 2¹/₂ miles. Coasters who wish to complete the entire Greensand Way may therefore wish to walk this stretch which is described in this book in Section 31A.

Hascombe Church. Section 34

Pitch Hill. Section 36

Leith Hill tower. Section 37

33: WORMLEY

The drive eventually bends L. Take a grassy path in front of the house with ponds R. One hundred yards after the ponds, take a path L into woods with a wall L. This goes up steps to a path. Turn R and, 30yds on, L up a steep path. Go over a X-track to a field. Cross this via three stiles to a road. Go through the gate opposite and along a fenced path. Before reaching the hedge of Heath Hall bear R to follow it round to a stile L. Descend steps to a lane. Go through the gate opposite and over a field to a stile. Cross the next field to a further stile. Here turn R, through a gate, to walk in front of the entrance to Lower House and through a kissing gate. Head straight downhill to a stile and then turn R up a dirt drive. At the top, the lane goes past the remains of a gate. Turn L just beyond a ridged boundary to a kissing gate. The path now descends to a kissing gate and a road. Turn L to a road. Cross this and walk up a metalled lane that becomes a woodland path. As the main route bends L, go R with woods R and fields L. This path runs for ¼ mile and bends L. Bear R near a metal gate along a woodland path to meet a road near The Hill House. Turn R at the next road junction. Follow this lane round past a junction R and Sandhills to a path R opposite Woodbury Cottage. Enter woodland and bear L near a seat down to a road. Cross to a dirt lane and turn L. The lane bears R through woods to a house. Walk on, crossing a minor road at one point, to go along a fenced path. This path crosses the railway near Witley Station. Continue to a road and turn R. Almost opposite The Pig & Whistle, turn L along a path. On reaching a road, turn L for 30yds and then R along a minor road. When the road bends sharp R, bear L along a track through woods to a house. Bear R in front of the house along a sandy path and then around L, following the curve of the hill past a school L. After passing an old concrete seat, bear L at a fork to reach a road. Turn L.

(OSL 186: OSP 1245) (4m/6.25km)

Waggoners Wells

Hascombe Pond

Ewhurst windmill

Earlswood Common

33: WORMLEY

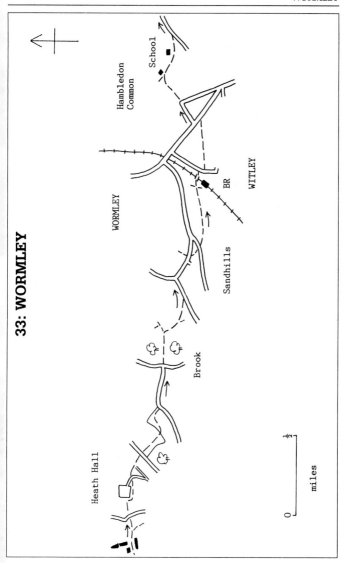

Heath Hall

Brook

Sandhills

WORMLEY

Hambledon Common

School

BR

WITLEY

0 ··· ½ miles

34: HASCOMBE

Follow the lane around a couple of bends and, just after Matteryes cottage, bear R up some steps to a stile. Bear R across the field with power lines R to another stile. Now head up the field towards a church on the horizon. Cross a stile into a lane. Turn R to pass St Peter's Church (with its fine yew tree) and on to a green lane. Follow this for about ½ mile to a T-jct. Turn R along an unmade drive and then, within 20yds, bear L along a narrow bridleway. (NB. Greensand Way route marked on OSP map is different here). This passes through woods near the edge of a field and bears R at a fork to go down a lane. Stay on the path, bearing L to go around Burgate Hanger. After about ½ mile, turn L along a road for about 75yds. Turn R along a gully and out onto Holloways Heath. Continue on a straight course for ⅔ mile to a point where the path starts to descend steeply. Here turn R and then almost immediately L (another path leaves R just here) to go downhill. In a little over 150yds, the main path bends R. Turn L along an indistinct track which descends rapidly. This leads to a field. Walk on with the hedge close R and over stile to a road near The White Horse pub at Hascombe. Turn L and bear R past the pub, heading to R of the church. Follow the road around R past the village pond R and St Peter's Church L. After the pond, the road bends L. Continue through a gate and into woods along a track. After ⅓ mile, bear L along a broad track to pass a barn (R) and enter a copse. At a X-track, turn L. This leads to a T-jct. Turn R here to reach a main track where you turn L to a road near Scotsland Farm. Turn R along the road and then, within 50yds, L on a path with a fence close L.

(OSL 186: OSP 1245/1246/1226) (4.25m/6.75km)

34: HASCOMBE

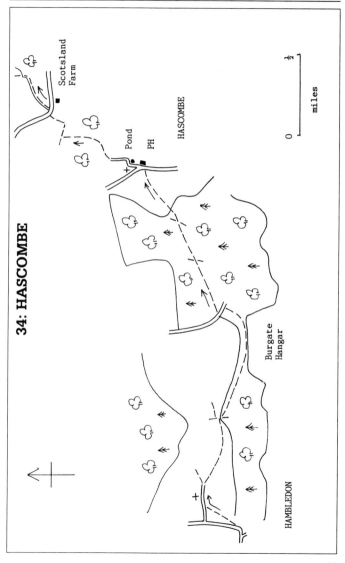

Scotsland Farm

Pond

PH

HASCOMBE

Burgate
Hangar

HAMBLEDON

0   ½

miles

35: SHAMLEY GREEN

The path continues through woods and goes L to open fields. Walk with fence L round to a dip. As the main path bends R towards a house, go straight up a slope with a fenced area to L and clump of pine trees R. Cross a drive and then a field - bearing R towards a barn (ie. to R of house). Go along drive through a gate and past a barn. Follow path round with copse R to a lane. Turn L to pass a house. The lane becomes a track. At a fork bear R to continue on to a lane. Turn L to pass a house L. When the lane turns sharp L, go straight on over a cattle grid. Cross a stile and continue on with fence close R. Go through a gate and out to a road. Turn L and, after 100yds, R into Rooks Hill Farm. The path goes through the farm, over an old railway and then the Wey & Arun Canal. Go straight to cross the small bridge and continue through two gates to a lane. Bear R past a telegraph pole to another gate. Walk on along a fenced path to a road at Shamley Green (turn L for pubs and buses). Go straight along a path to R of the church. This becomes a fenced path along the L edge of a field. At a T-jct, turn R to another T-jct for another R turn into Little Cucknells. Pass the house L and walk on to cross a stile. Go along the R edge of a field. After another stile, the path descends to a road at Stroud Farm. Turn R and then, after 100yds, L towards Franklins. Continue past the house and, in 150yds, turn L. Cross a stile to go through trees and over a field (pond R) to a stile in the corner. Go up a slope to a stile. Bear R of centre to go along path with fence close R to a T-jct. Turn R along a forest drive. When the main track goes R, bear L up bridleway into newly planted woods. After $^{1}/_{4}$ mile, the path joins a bigger track. Bear R along a path strewn with brick rubble to a road. Bear L up some steps. Keep R along the edge of a car park onto a path which enters Winterfold Forest. Continue through heather, gorse and birch; avoiding paths off.

(OSL 186/187: OSP 1226) (5.25m/8.5km)

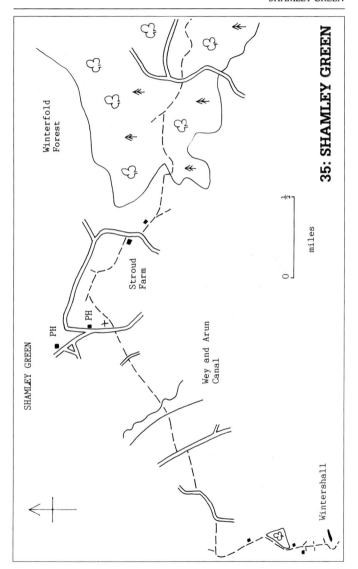

35: SHAMLEY GREEN

Winterfold
Forest

Stroud
Farm

PH

PH

SHAMLEY GREEN

Wey and Arun
Canal

Wintershall

0

miles

36: PITCH HILL

After passing a car park L, continue on for 250yds and turn sharp L (the path straight on is blocked by a fallen tree). This new path goes through trees, over a drive and out to a road. Turn R to pass Jelleys Hollow to take a path R which initially runs parallel with the road. The path moves away and then back to the road before bending R to a viewpoint on Reynards Hill. It then winds back L to reach another car park. Turn R along the road for a short distance to a junction. Go straight on up a track. After passing Ewhust windmill, bear R downhill to cross the road to a car park. Just after the entrance, turn R to go up to Pitch Hill trig point. Carry on past the column and turn L. The path winds around the edge of the hill to a seat. About 50yds further on, bear R downhill. Turn L onto a dirt drive. Pass a house and then, 300yds further on, turn R along a path which goes over a X-track to a gap in the fence and down to the drive of the Duke of Kent School. Walk out to the road and bear L to a fenced path. Go along this for $^1/_2$ mile. At end bear R to pass a gate to a T-jct. Turn L along a path and go R at a fork to reach a road. Cross the road into a car park. Keep to the R edge and just before reaching a barrier, go R along an indistinct path which goes over a gully and up some steps. The main path now winds up the hill to reach a memorial seat on the top of Holmbury Hill Fort. Turn L down a slope. This track runs on for $^1/_3$ mile to a point where there are a series of X-tracks. Turn first R to follow a path which goes past a cricket ground and, eventually, out to road. Turn L along road and then bear R (bear L for choice of two pubs) along Pitland Street. At the end of this road, turn R (bus stops here for Guildford and Dorking). After 50yds turn L to walk uphill along a road to a point where it swings R near a white house. Here turn R up a bridleway through Pasture Wood.

(OSL 187: OSP 1226) (5m/8km)

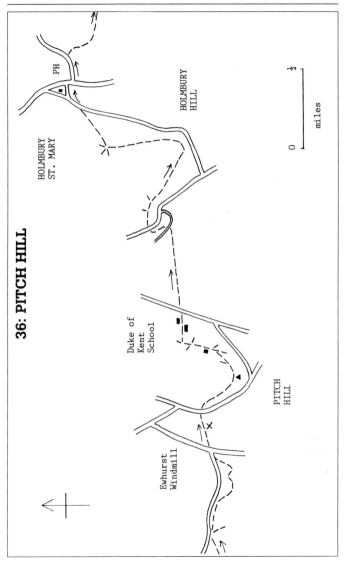

36: PITCH HILL

HOLMBURY ST. MARY

PH

HOLMBURY HILL

Duke of Kent School

PITCH HILL

Ewhurst Windmill

0   ½

miles

37: LEITH HILL

The clear woodland path continues for nearly a mile through storm ravaged landscape to High Ashes Farm. Shortly after passing the buildings L, the dirt drive reaches a T-jct. Turn R. After about 50yds, the main drive goes R. We meanwhile go straight on along an equally wide track uphill. This leads to another T-jct near two gates. Turn L to go uphill to a road. Bear R across the road and then L (following a bridleway sign to The Tower) to continue along a path through woodland. This reaches Leith Hill Tower in $1/2$ mile. Continue past the tower to go downhill. At the bottom turn L at a X-track just before Dukes Warren. This dirt track (later a dirt drive) continues for $1^1/2$ miles to a lane near the Triple Bar Riding Centre. Turn R along the lane for a few yards and then bear R along a wide path into the Wotton Estate. Follow this path, past some ponds (and the River Tillingbourne), a waterfall and the occasional house, for about $1^1/4$ miles. At the lane, turn R to pass a house and then R again to follow a path that runs L of a muddy track (do not take the footpath L here). At the end, bear R into the track and then L into another storm ravaged wood. This path winds around the fallen trees and downhill with fine views R to the ponds of Pipp Brook. Bear L along the track at the bottom of the hill which passes houses L to reach a metalled drive in front of the entrance to The Rookery. Turn R to walk along the drive past houses to reach the A25. Turn R to go up a sandy path and into woods. At a lane turn R to a T-jct. Here turn L and then R along a path with a small cemetery to the R. Continue over a drive and down a path with houses to L. At the end bear R with houses on both sides to a metal kissing gate and a fenced path. In $1/2$ mile, this path goes up and then down to a house and a footbridge over a brook. Turn L along the lane and then within 100yds R up some steps.

(OSL 187: OSP 1226) (6.5m/10.5km)

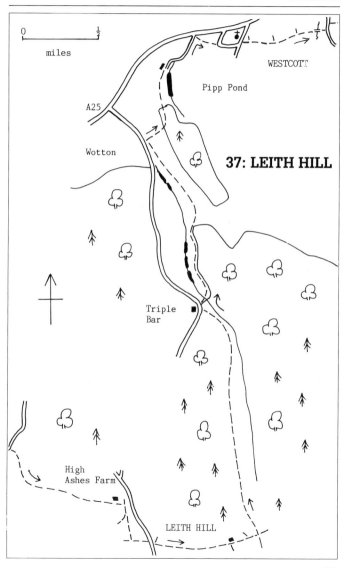

0

miles

½

WESTCOTT

Pipp Pond

A25

Wotton

37: LEITH HILL

Triple
Bar

High
Ashes Farm

LEITH HILL

38: DORKING

Continue along a fenced path to a lane. Turn L. After 200yds, the lane bends L. Take a path R, bearing R at a fork to go up to a seat and shelter. Go along a grass path for $^1/_4$ mile to a seat. Turn L downhill to the far R corner of a field. Turn R through a gate and over a road. Turn L up Nower Road and then R at the telephone box to descend to a main road. Cross the road effectively to bear R to The Queen's Head (for central Dorking turn L). Go up the alley to R of pub. At a T-jct, turn R and, at the road, L. Where the road goes R, continue along road with St Paul's Church L. After 250yds, turn R along a path with a school L. Go through a gate and uphill into Glory Wood. Turn immediately L along a path through trees. At a fork, go L eventually to reach the A24. Continue ahead to cross Chart Lane, then cross the A24 to a concrete lane. This turns R and goes uphill with the A24 R. After 200yds turn L uphill. At the top, go straight on to a lane. Follow this downhill past houses and turn R at two successive T-jcts. The road enters open country to reach the entrance to Park Farm. Turn L through a kissing gate to walk along the drive. When you reach buildings go straight on along a track which winds around a pond and under the railway. The path continues to R of centre between fields. At the end of a small copse to R, turn R and then L to cross a stile. Walk on with a hedge close L, through a gate and on to the top L corner of the field. Cross the stile and turn L following the L edge of a field to a further stile. Cross the lane and go straight on to cross two stiles to a wide green lane. Turn R to walk into Brockham (shops, pubs and buses). Cross the green to R of pump and on past The Duke's Head. Go along the lane and before the gates, turn L along a path. After crossing the River Mole, turn R. In 150yds where the main lane goes L, bear R onto a path with river R. This path passes houses L and goes into pasture.

(OSL 187: OSP 1226/1227) (5m/8km)

38: DORKING

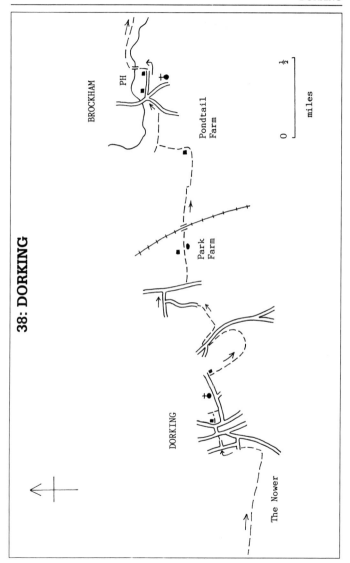

BROCKHAM

PH

Pondtail
Farm

Park
Farm

DORKING

The Nower

0 miles ½

39: BETCHWORTH

At the end of a field, go along a fenced path and through two gates to go R of St Michael's Church to a road and The Dolphin. Continue along Wonham Lane. After passing a pond, take a path L along the R edge of a field. At the end turn L along Sandy Lane to a T-jct. Turn R and R again up steps. Cross a stile and bear L over a field to cross another stile. Turn immediately R through a gate and then L over a further stile. Continue, with hedge L, to a kissing gate and on with fence close R. This rises to a gate to L of Juniper Cottage. Go along an alley to a track and turn R. This winds past Dungates Farm to cross a brook. As the main track bends L, go R through a gate, over a field and through a further gate. Walk on to a cottage (L) and a golf course. Cross the fairway towards a sandy path that rises to R of a windmill. Go up this path and along a lane. After passing a bungalow and before the lane bends L, turn R downhill over a series of rides. Cross a road and go along the lane opposite. This leads to a path which skirts the edge of woods with houses L. On reaching a small area surrounded by cottages, head to the L corner to enter a pathway. This leads to The Skimmington Castle. Walk past the pub and over a drive to descend a short distance to a path. Turn R along this to a metalled lane. Turn L to go uphill to a T-jct. Cross the road and go up steps. Go over a X-path and on uphill into Priory Park. Follow a grass ridge for $^1/_2$ mile. Go R of a trig point and a seat to go down through trees. At a tarmac path, turn L and descend to a road (A217). Turn R. Cross the road at bollards and go uphill over St Mary's Road. After Lymden Gardens, bear L up Isbells Drive. At the top, turn L to go along a path to a suburban road. Turn L. After passing Orewell Road L, take a path which goes R with garages L. This leads down to a barrier. Turn L. The path now winds through woods. Avoid all X-tracks and paths R to keep roughly straight on.

(OSL 187: OSP 1227/1207) (4.5m/7km)

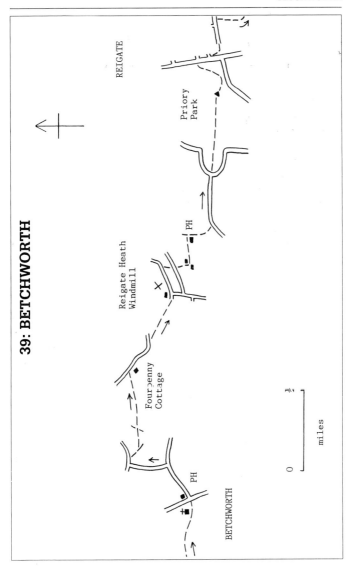

39: BETCHWORTH

REIGATE

Priory
Park

Reigate Heath
Windmill

PH

Four Penny
Cottage

PH

BETCHWORTH

miles

0

Surrey's Villages to the Fore

There's no doubting that Surrey is a pretty crowded place. After all, as cricket fans know, the Kennington Oval is in Surrey and you can't get more embedded in the metropolis than that. And yet here, in the same county, is some of the most refreshing countryside in the whole country. Maybe it's the sheer proximity to the city that makes it so welcome. Maybe it's the relief that comes with escaping from same that makes it so rewarding. None of it is very wild of course. Indeed, you could say that's it's all a little manicured. But it is well...nice countryside. It's the stuff that model railway layouts are made of. There's nothing desolate or nasty. It's cultured, civilised stuff for cultured, civilised folk.

We enter the "wilds" of Surrey at Hindhead, the highest village in the county at 850ft above sea level. It's a popular place for a Sunday afternoon out. Here people arrive, wander about for half an hour, have an ice cream or a cup of tea and go home in time to see The Antiques Road Show. They come to see the Devil's Punch Bowl, a deep valley to the left of the old Portsmouth Road as we walk along it. They also come to see Gibbet Hill, the place where three murderers were hanged in 1786. Whatever else can be said about this event, they must have had a great view.

Surrey has the kind of villages that dreams are made of: the broad green where leather hits willow, the village pub with the friendly landlord, the local shop with the chatty helpful shopkeeper and the rose fronted cottages with the old boy who knows a decent compost when he sees one. Yes, this is the life. And you'll walk through a whole series of such villages on the Greensand Way: Hascombe with its pond, Shamley with its village green, Holmbury St Mary with its hillside cricket pitch, Brockham with its village pump and Betchworth who's pub, the Dolphin, serves Young's wonderful Winter Warmer in front of a roaring log fire. The list could go on. Yet these villages are only the interludes between the hills. We scale Pitch Hill and then Reynards Hill which sports

Ewhurst windmill - infamous in its working days for its role in the distribution of contraband en route from the coast to London. At Holmbury Hill there is an iron age hill fort as well as a convenient memorial seat. The Nower at Dorking also has fine views as well as a memorial seat of its own. Priory Park has a view down to Reigate and, yes you've guessed it, a memorial seat. The most famous hill of all is Leith Hill which is 965ft above sea level, a height that tops the 1,000 if you scale the 64ft high tower (National Trust and open on appropriate occasions). The guidebooks say that the tower was built by Richard Hull in 1766. He liked it so much that he had himself interned underneath. Nowadays he would never have been allowed to do either. Such is progress.

The frequent villages means that pubs are common enough to allow coasters to stagger from one to another at will. They can be found at: Hindhead, Thursley (Three Horseshoes in GPG), Brook (turn R along A288), Hascombe (White Horse in GPG), Shamley Green (turn L at Christchurch for Red Lion in GPG), Holmbury St Mary (Kings Head in GPG), Westcott (turn R at A25 for Cricketers), Dorking (CAMRA & GPG list the Cricketers), Brockham (Royal Oak in GPG), Betchworth (Dolphin in CAMRA & GPG), Reigate Heath (Skimmington Castle in GPG), Reigate (turn L at A217 for CAMRA listed Yew Tree), Redhill (turn L at A23), Bletchingly (on A25: GPG lists all 3 pubs), Tandridge, Broadham Green and Limpsfield Chart (Carpenter's Arms). Small shops are less common so stock up. They will be found at Hindhead, Shamley Green, Brockham, South Nutfield and Bletchingly. Dorking (close), Reigate (1/2 mile north) and Redhill (a mile north) are major shopping centres with all the usual multiples as well as a choice of cafes and restaurants.

40: REDHILL

Eventually the path climbs a steep sandy track to reach a fork. Bear L and follow path round R. Then go straight on with houses L to fenced path and road. Turn R downhill. Cross the road and go L along Cronks Hill Road. After bending R and passing Dunotter Close, turn L into an alley which passes houses R to reach Earlswood Common (for Redhill go L). Turn R to cross road near bus stop. Bear away from road onto golf course. Go straight on with trees L. At a fork, bear R with small copse L to a tee. Here bear L through trees to an embankment. Turn L past toilets and on with lake R. Keep this line past a tee and out to a road. Turn L and, after 200yds, R into Royal Earlswood Hospital. Go under railway and bear L through gate into and through hospital grounds. At end, go straight on along a road. When this goes R continue on path with fence and field L to Redhill Brook. Turn R over stile and bear R to another stile. In next field, go diagonally across to stile. Now head to L of an old house to concrete drive. At the corner of field, turn R to follow hedge to its end and then go L, aiming R of two power cable poles to cross stile. Turn L along concrete road. After 20yds, go R over field passing to R of oak tree. Go through hedge gap and on with hedge L to road. Turn L past Kings Mill and Mill Cottage. Bear R along old road and go up Bowerhill Lane which goes under the railway and turns R. Before descending a hill, turn R past barrier and along path to cross stile. The path bears L, goes over stile and along fenced path to road. Turn R past school and shop. At Cobbers, turn L along drive to go over stile to field. Follow L field edge to corner where bear L through hedge to walk the R edge of next field. Cross two stiles and turn L with hedge L. Go up hill, over stile and bear R to top R corner of field. Cross stile and turn R down road. After passing Brewing Research Foundation car park, turn L along drive to Colgates Barn Cottages.

(OSL 187: OSP 1227) (5.5m/8.75km)

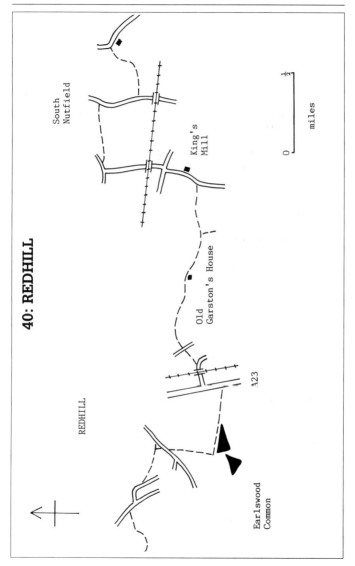

40: REDHILL

REDHILL

South
Nutfield

King's
Mill

Old
Garston's House

A23

Earlswood
Common

0   ½
miles

41: BLETCHINGLY

The Colgates Barn Cottages drive goes through a gate and under the M23. Follow the clear drive around through parkland for about ¹/₂ mile. At a barn, bear L to a gate and then turn R up a fenced path. Half a mile further on, the route reaches a road (turn L here for Bletchingly pubs, shops and buses to Reigate and Westerham). The walk continues over the road and along the path opposite with a house wall close R. At the next road, turn R and then L into the entrance of Bletchingly Quarry. Within 20yds, turn L along a path. After 250yds, turn R to follow a hedge close R over a concrete road to another path which runs for nearly ¹/₂ mile to a road. Bear L onto the road. Where it turns L, go straight on along a dirt drive onto Tilburstow Hill. After ¹/₄ mile, this reaches another road. Turn L to follow the lane round R for 200yds. Turn R along a path which follows the edge of Tilburstow Woods. Go over a X-track and on to where the main path goes L. Here we go through a gate and over a field to a path which leads to a road. Cross to another path which, after ¹/₄ mile, bends L. Ignore the tempting stile R and go on to a gate. Just before reaching it, turn R to go over a stile and straight across a field. In the middle of the field is, curiously, a waymarker post. This points us slightly L out to a stile and down, via a small field, to a road. Turn L to walk on to Godstone. At the first road turning R there is a triangular traffic island. Turn R here to pass Leigh Mill House via a ford bridge. The path continues on through a kissing gate with a pond down R to the A22 Godstone by-pass. Cross with care and continue directly over to another path which goes along field edges for about ¹/₂ mile to Tandridge.

(OSL 187: OSP 1207/1227) (5m/8km)

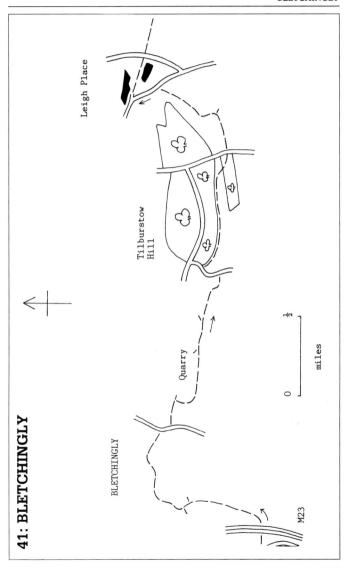

41: BLETCHINGLY

Leigh Place

Tilburstow
Hill

Quarry

BLETCHINGLY

M23

0                    $\frac{1}{2}$

miles

42: LIMPSFIELD

The path continues along field edges to Tandridge. Turn R along the road and then first L past the Barley Mow pub. This minor road bends L and then R before continuing along a path which starts to R of some garages. Go over a stile and along the L-hand edge of a field and through a kissing gate near a barn. Turn R and follow path across Tandridge Park. Eventually the path joins a metalled drive to go downhill, over a X-track and out to a road at Broadham Green. Turn L and then R along Tanhouse Road to reach The Haycutter. Turn L over a stile opposite the pub. The clear path winds around the fields and over several stiles to reach Oxted Mill and a road. Turn R to go uphill to a T-jct. Turn L for a short distance and then R along a track. This path runs through Oxted suburbia for ¹/₄ mile before reaching a drive. At a T-jct, turn L to reach another T-jct. Here cross the road to go up a fenced path and on to Limpsfield Common. Keep L to walk along the metalled drive and to pass St Michael's Girls School. Just opposite the school entrance cross the road and go along a path into woods. Cross the next road into a car park and then bear L along a track. In an open area, take a R fork and continue along the path over the common for just over ¹/₄ mile to a drive and a T-jct. Turn R for 100yds and, just after Links Cottages, bear L on a path through scrub, over a golf course and out to a road in front of Pains Hill Chapel. Take the path to the L of the chapel to a road and turn L. At the end of the road, go L along a gravel driveway. This goes past some cottages and over a drive to reach a road and a bus stop. Cross the road and turn R along the pavement. Go over the next road and continue roughly straight on to walk past the front of the Carpenters Arms pub.

(OSL 187: OSP 1207/1208) (4.5m/7km)

42: LIMPSFIELD

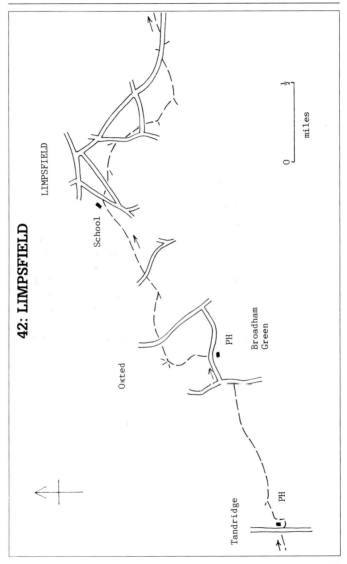

43: TOYS HILL

At a T-jct, go straight on into woods. In 250yds, turn L near a waymark along a path that leads over two X-paths and ahead on a narrow path onto a common. This reaches a broad dirt drive. Turn L for 100yds to a spot where paths intersect. Bear R to go along a path which starts with paling fencing R. Go along a fenced path to a road. Continue downhill. In 150yds, turn R along a track which goes through rhododendrons to cross a stile near a gate. Go along the drive past Kent House Lodge. After 100yds turn L and bear R along a path which crosses a drive. Bear L at one fork and R at a second to walk on to a road. Turn L and bear L up a partially metalled drive. This leads to a house with a mini-roundabout. Bear R across the front of the house and straight on to a valley. Bear R to a drive and then L to a road. Bear R to a track to R of the entrance to Windmill Bank. This rises to join a path. Bear L with fence R for 20yds, then turn L and cross a metalled lane onto a broad path. Stay on this (avoiding turns L) to a road near Chartwell car park. Continue along a fenced path opposite and go uphill across a road and along another track. This clear path bends L with beech trees R. After passing a tennis court, turn R onto a drive and then R immediately onto a path. This descends to a road at French Street. Turn R and, after ¹/₂ mile, bear R towards some buildings. Go past the entrance and continue with a high fence R onto Toys Hill. At a T-jct turn R and follow the path that twists and turns for ¹/₄ mile. When you reach a single cross bar gate, bear L and follow the track to a road. Turn L. Opposite a National Trust car park, turn R onto a path near a National Trust notice. The path bends L. After 250yds, bear R. Keep on this track, ignoring paths off as it descends to a stile and a field. Turn L, with hedge close L, to another stile. Cross and bear R to a stile near a gate. Continue across next field to a bridge in the far R corner. Cross the brook and turn L along the L field edge.

(OSL 187/188: OSP 1208) (5m/8km)

43: TOYS HILL

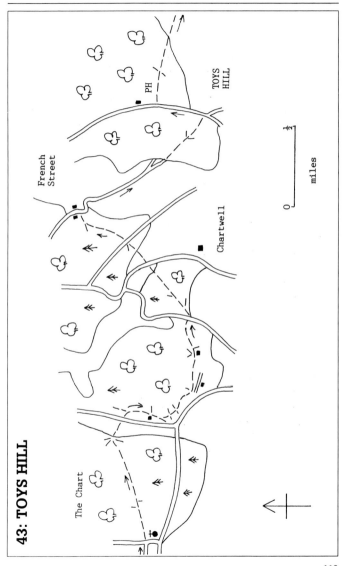

The Chart

PH

French
Street

TOYS
HILL

Chartwell

0   ½

miles

44: SEVENOAKS WEALD

Continue to a farm track which, after crossing several fields, reaches The Crown at Ide Hill. Turn R then L to pass the Cock Inn. The road bends R to a junction. Turn R (to R of The Churchill) and, after 15yds, go L uphill to an open space. Go straight along a marked path. Bear R soon after starting but otherwise stay on the path which leads to a car park. Cross the lane and go along a path parallel to a road L. Fifty yards after a small parking area, go R downhill to a field and fence that push the path L over a stile. Cross two fields and two stiles into woods. A path then leads to a field. Go half R to meet a path which runs along the L field edge. Just before Hatchlands Farm, turn L over a stile. Bear R over a bridge to a stile and road. Turn L for 100yds and then R over a stile. Go downhill with hedge L. When this goes L, bear towards buildings. Cross a stile in the field corner and go along drive with Wickhurst Manor L. After the drive turns L, go R over a stile and up the field to a second stile. Now bear L to go L of farm buildings. Cross two stiles and go down the field and over a brook. The path continues up a slope to a gap. Cross a stile into a field and walk towards an oast house. Cross the fence that surrounds the farmyard via a stile (to L of brick barn). At end of barn, turn R and then L past the oast house. Leave the farm and bear L over a stile and down a field to cross a brook. Go uphill, under cables and over a stile. Go along the R field edge to a stile and road (turn L here for Sevenoaks). Turn R and take the L fork to reach Sevenoaks Weald. Just before houses L, turn L to a stile. Cross the field to the far corner. Turn R on the metalled lane and then L just before a barn. The track bends R then L to go under the Sevenoaks by-pass. At the tunnel end, go over a stile and turn L through a gate. Continue alongside the by-pass up a slope. On the brow of the hill, a waymark on the fence points R. Go up the hill and bear L with fence R, to cross a stile. Turn R along a hedged track for ²/₃ mile.

(OSL 188: OSP 1208) (5m/8km)

44: SEVENOAKS WEALD

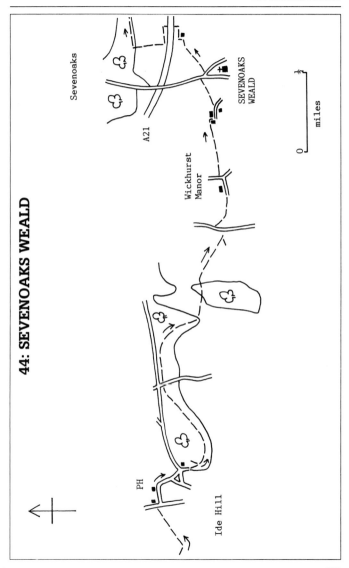

Sevenoaks

A21

Wickhurst
Manor

SEVENOAKS
WEALD

Ide Hill

PH

miles

0

45: ONE TREE HILL

The track leads to a road. Cross to a pavement and walk uphill for 250yds. Turn R along a minor road. At the top of the hill, go L through a gate into Knole Park. Follow the Broad Walk to a fork R onto the long straight Chestnut Walk. Follow this for $^2/_3$ mile. The walk undulates. At the second dip, there are two concrete hydrant posts facing each other to R. At the third dip, there is just one and it's facing the path. Turn R here to a gate. Cross the road to a path that goes through a wood to a stile and a field. Bear R slightly to pass a dressage arena and walk on to a stile in the far R corner. The path now descends to a drive and a road. Turn L for 150yds then turn R into One Tree Hill. The path goes up to an open area with a concrete seat. Bear L to the far corner and take the path onwards which leads L to a T-jct. Turn R to a large beech tree and a fence. Turn R so that the fence is to L. This path descends through woods with a steep slope R to arrive at Rooks Hill Cottage. Turn R down a minor road and, after 150yds, turn L into woodland. Cross a stile and continue through woods and out to open ground with a fence, field and views R. At the field end, the path bends R to go over a stile and down steps. Turn L in front of Wilmot Cottage and out via a gate to an unmade drive. Follow this for $^3/_4$ mile to pass Mote Farm with four oast houses. Turn L to a road and R to pass the entrance of Ightham Mote. At the corner of a field near a road bends sign, cross a stile L and walk on with hedge close R. Cross a stile and bear L over the field to a further stile. This path goes through woods, over a X-track to a stile into a field. A clear path descends to the edge of some woodland and a young conifer planting. Here turn L towards a yellow waymark post and the corner of the field. Turn R and go over the field to a yellow post. Cross the stile in the corner of the next field and walk on with hedge close L to a gate in the church wall.

(OSL 188: OSP 1208) (5m/8km)

45: ONE TREE HILL

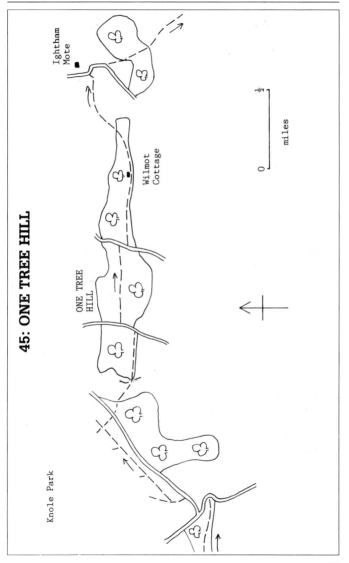

Knole Park

ONE TREE
HILL

Wilmot
Cottage

Ightham
Mote

miles

46: SHIPBOURNE COMMON

Walk around Shipbourne Church and through the lychgate to a road near The Chaser pub. Walk up the road opposite which bisects the common until it bends R near a white house. To the R of the house is a track which leads to a stile and a field. Walk on with a fence close R. When this turns R, go straight on towards a farm lane which goes uphill. At the top, go straight on past Fairlawne Home Farm onto a drive to a road. Cross this to go over a stile and straight on into woods via a stile. Bear L to a stile and then go straight over the next field to a further stile. Don't cross this but turn R to follow the field edge to a stile. Cross here and follow the R-hand edge of the field to a gate and a road. Turn L and then R to go along Roughway Lane, passing The Kentish Rifleman. This lane bends L over a brook. At the end of a row of houses, the road bends L. Here cross a stile R and walk into the field with the fence close R. As this bends R, continue on the same course over a field. When you reach a hedge, turn R and descend to a footbridge over a brook. Keep the fence close L until you reach a stile in it. Cross into the next field and follow the brook up to a second bridge. Cross this and head slightly L away from the brook towards an oast house that has a waymark sign on its outer fence. Bear L to a gate. Cross two stiles to a road. Turn L for 20yds then R onto a hedged path which passes a house and goes on to a gate. Continue straight on to another stile. Walk along the R edge of the field to the end where a gap R leads to a farm lane. Turn L and go down the lane to a road. Turn L and, after 20yds, go R behind some white railings. This leads to a stile and a field. Walk on with a hedge and then a stand of poplar trees L. At the end, just before a bungalow, bear L onto a track. Go through a gate, across West Peckham village green and along a road with the church L and The Swan R.

(OSL 188: OSP 1208/1209) (4m/6.5km)

46: SHIPBOURNE COMMON

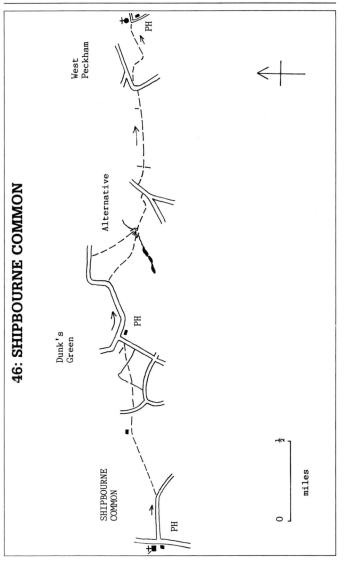

Carpenter's Arms, Limpsfield Chart. Section 42

Ightham Mote. Section 45

Right through Kent to the Coast

Kent was ravaged by the great storm of October 1987 and is only just beginning to recover. Whole swathes of woodland were destroyed and many of the victims still lie where they fell. Luckily the decimation hasn't entirely spoilt the beauty of the place and hopefully it will recuperate. There has been a massive programme of replanting and nature is fighting back. After all, these Kentish soils have a reputation for high fertility and soon, we hope, the place will return to its former glory. You should be able to check it out as the Southern Coast to Coast goes through many of the devastated woods. Toys Hill, Ide Hill, One Tree Hill (almost literally) and Rooks Hill have all suffered. Further into the county however, we see that many of the orchards have been damaged as well and a number have had to be restocked.

The Southern Coast to Coast in Kent also has its own fair share of culture. The route passes a series of stately homes between Westerham and Maidstone including three National Trust properties (all of which serve great tea and cakes!). Chartwell near Westerham was the country home of Sir Winston Churchill from 1922 until his death in 1965. The house can get crowded but there are many exhibits on the great man as well as curiosities such as the brick wall that he built in the garden. Knole near Sevenoaks is a massive fifteenth-century country house that was enlarged in 1603 by Thomas Sackville. It has a number of silk and velvet tapestries and numerous paintings by Gainsborough and Reynolds. Ightham Mote is a medieval moated manor house. The Old Chapel and Crypt date from about 1340 and a modern extension - a drawing room - was built in the eighteenth century. All these properties are worth a visit if you have time.

We also pass through a series of fine villages that compete hard with those of Surrey. Both West Peckham and Shipbourne (pronounced "shibburn") have fine pubs and splendid village greens. Yalding has two fifteenth-century bridges. Boughton Monchelsea has a greystone Elizabethan manor set in a seventy-nine-acre deer park. Sutton Valence is home to an imposing public school, founded in 1576. Whilst the highly attractive villages of Egerton and Pluckley have shot to public attention as the home (on TV at least) of Pop Larkin in *The Darling Buds of May*.

Shops are few and far between on our route through Kent but pubs are common enough. Just north of the National Trust car park at Toy's Hill you'll find the Fox & Hounds (CAMRA) and Ide Hill has both the Crown and the Cock Inn (both GPG). Sevenoaks Weald has the Chequer Tree, Shipbourne has the Chaser (GPG), Dunk's Green has the Kentish Rifleman, West Peckham has the Swan and Nettlestead Green has the Hop Pole. Yalding isn't a big place but it has a range of shops and pubs (GPG lists the Walnut Tree). After Linton (Bull Inn), the next convenient hostelry is the Kings Head at Sutton Valence. Pepper Box (GPG) and The Harrier are at Ulcombe. There's a small shop and the George Inn at Egerton and another small shop and the Black Horse at Pluckley. We pass the Swan Inn at Little Chart, CAMRA recommend the Hooden Horse at Great Chart and there's the Queen's Head at Kingsnorth.

St Nicholas' Church, Boughton Malherbe. Section 51

Nettlestead Green

Linton

Barn Hill Farm near Coxheath. Section 48

The George Inn and St James' Church, Egerton. Section 51

The coast into Dover (left)

47: NETTLESTEAD GREEN

Walk past houses to Mereworth Road and on to Dukes Place Farmhouse hidden behind a conifer hedge. Turn R down a concrete lane. As this bends R, go straight through a gate and over a field to a metal farm gate. Don't go through this but bear R to a stile 100yds short of the field corner. Cross a stile and follow the path over a footbridge and another stile into a field. Bear L to the far corner of the field where, after going over two stiles, a drive leads to the A26. Turn R for 50yds and then L up a lane. This crosses a road and goes uphill to East Peckham Old Church. Go up some steps to enter the churchyard and round to R of the church. Bear R to a gap in the wall and continue down a slope to a stile. Cross and bear L downhill through an orchard. Continue with a fence close L and on over two stiles. Follow the track round and over an area of parkland to a gate opposite Roydon Hall. Turn R and walk along the lane for 250yds to a cottage. Turn L through the yard and over a stile. Walk on with the fence close L for $^1/_3$ mile to a stile into woods. The path goes through various plantations including an area of conifers to reach a path T-jct. Turn R through more recent planting to a stile. Head over the centre of the field to a gap in the trees ahead. This leads to a field. Turn L. At the corner of the wood, continue across the field towards the houses ahead. Cross a stile L so that the hedge is to R. Cross a further stile and follow a path between houses to a road. Cross the stile opposite and walk on over the field to a stile R. Take a diagonal course across the next field, 30° R of the poplar trees on the horizon. Cross the railway and turn R with the Medway L. At the road, turn L over a bridge and on alongside the canal over another bridge. Turn L onto The Lees and head towards a large oak tree. Cross the footbridge and walk on to reach the road and central Yalding. Turn L. After the Two Brewers, go L past The Bull (L). Turn R into Vicarage Road then L along a metalled path.

(OSL 188: OSP 1209/1229) (4.75m/7.5km)

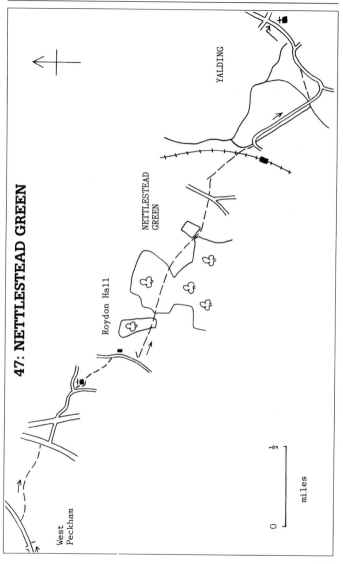

47: NETTLESTEAD GREEN

YALDING

NETTLESTEAD
GREEN

Roydon Hall

West
Peckham

0   ½   miles

48: LINTON

This path leads to a road in a housing estate. Ignore the GW waymark for the easier route which is to walk straight on into Mount Avenue. Follow the road as it turns R and, at the end, take the path which bears L into countryside. This eventually reaches a road. Turn R and then, after 300yds, L along a bridleway. Walk up this muddy path for nearly $^1/_3$ mile and then R through a gap to follow the hedge L. This path continues to pass to the R of Buston Manor and on through the farmyard to the L of some oast houses. When the metalled track bends L, go straight on (to L of telegraph pole). This path skirts a wood to R and before reaching the next hedge, turn L at a waymark post. Head uphill to R of a scrubby area and turn L at the top, up a steep bank and over a stile. Turn R to walk on over two stiles to a road. Turn R past the entrance to Oak House and Oak Hill Cottages. Turn L along a farm track which runs about 150yds to the south of the cottages. This reaches a fence and bends L around a wire fence and before turning R onto a path which runs along the edge of an orchard. At the top of the slope, go L through a gap to a road. Turn R into the gulley and then L up some steps into an orchard. Walk on with the orchard to R. After 400yds, bear R at a fork. This leads to a X-track where we turn R for 10yds and then L over a stile to go on with a hedge to L. The way then bends L and R and then L again eventually to reach a road. Cross and bear L to another clear path. This leads to a bridge over Vanity Lane and an orchard. Go through the trees using the series of small, yellow-banded posts to guide the way. This leads to a path along the L edge of an overgrown orchard and out to another well-kempt one. Again follow the small posts through the trees and out to the busy A229. Turn R to Linton and The Bull Inn. Take the path which runs around the R-hand side of St Nicolas' Church to a kissing gate and a fenced path.

(OSL 188: OSP 1209) (4.5m/7km)

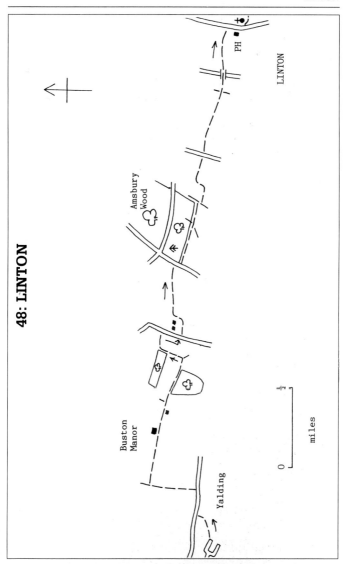

48: LINTON

Amsbury Wood

Buston Manor

Yalding

LINTON

PH

0   ½

miles

49: BOUGHTON MONCHELSEA

Follow the fenced path across the drive to Linton Park and on to a road at Loddington Oast. Continue straight on through orchards until, just before reaching a road and some buildings, the path goes L for 100yds and down some steps to a road. This is Boughton Monchelsea. Go along the path opposite which bears L through some woodland into a field. Bear R to go through a gate, over a drive and on along a path between fields to a stile. Our way now continues straight on to a stile and a kissing gate. Cross the drive to go through another kissing gate and to bear L over a stile to a further kissing gate and a road. Turn R for 30yds and then L along East Hall Hill. As the road bends R, go L through a gate into an orchard. Turn R with the hedge to R and walk on to go down some steps to a dirt drive. Turn L and follow the track as it runs a straight course between orchards to reach a stile. Go down some steep steps to a green lane. Turn R and keep L at the fork. When the main track goes R, go straight on. This path leads to a long series of steps down to a fence. Turn L and follow the path R to skirt around the orchard. At the far corner cross a plank bridge and walk on along a grassy path between rows of trees. Turn R at the top to follow the L-hand edge of the orchard through a farm gate to a road. Walk on along Chart Hill for nearly ¹/₂ mile to a road junction. Turn L along Church Road and, after 100yds, R towards St Michael and All Angels Church. Keep the church to R and turn R to walk a clear path which leads out to the A274 at Sutton Valence.

(OSL 188: OSP 1209/1229/1230) (4m/6.25km)

49: BOUGHTON MONCHELSEA

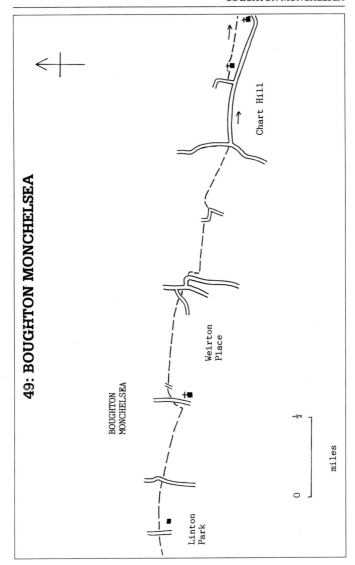

BOUGHTON
MONCHELSEA

Chart Hill

Weirton
Place

Linton
Park

0 $\frac{1}{2}$

miles

50: ULCOMBE

Turn R and then (before reaching the King's Head) L along path signposted to Tower House Lane. This path goes past Sutton Valence School into a playing field. Keep to the R-hand side and follow a path that descends to a road. Turn L and walk on for $^{1}/_{4}$ mile to a crossroads. Here take a path which leaves L from the crossing over a stile. Go diagonally over the field through a row of trees and out to a road near a signpost. Walk straight on along the road, past the church and prison for about $^{1}/_{2}$ mile. At a T-jct, go straight on through a gate and follow the path down the hill and through two gates. At the bottom of the valley bear R up to some old hop-pickers huts and then bear L out to a gate and a road. After a little more than 100yds, turn R past Morry Cottage. Walk on with hop gardens to both sides. As the metalled lane goes L, carry straight on. The path goes through a hedge and bears L to go along the L edge of an orchard onto a path which leads past a church (L) to a road. (Turn R here for pub in Ulcombe.) Go along the path directly opposite which goes across some scrubby land. Keep to the R edge of the field eventually to reach a stile into a field. Keep straight on uphill to a stile and another field. Here continue in the same direction uphill, down into a slight hollow and then up again to follow the path to the L of a row of trees. Walk on to cross a stile and to head across the centre of the next field. On reaching the hedge turn L to go uphill to a stile in the corner. Go over the stile, down some steps and turn L to go uphill to a road. Turn L to go past the entrances of two farms. About 100yds further on, go over the stile R and walk on with a hedge to L. The path leads to a lane. Cross to another path bearing L to a stile in the top L corner of the field.

(OSL 188/189: OSP 1230) (4m/6.25km)

50: ULCOMBE

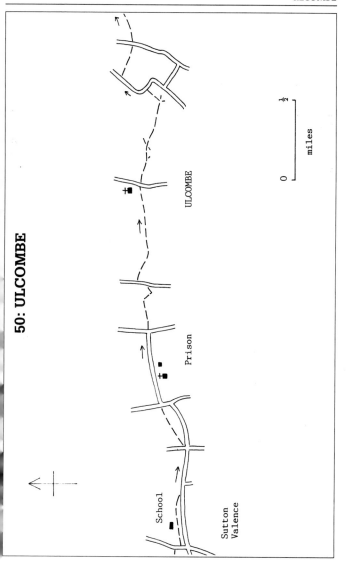

51: EGERTON

Bear L through a wood to a stile and a road. Turn L and then R onto a broad grass track. Cross a stile into an orchard. Cross a second stile to a road and on to another orchard. Bear L along a row of trees (a notice points the way). Go through the hedge at the end and down a slope to a field. Go on through an alley to the road at Liverton Street. Cross the road and go up steps to an enclosed path. Follow this to a stile into a field and walk on with hedge L. Bear R through farm buildings and then L to a road. Walk on with St Nicholas' Church, Boughton Malherbe, L. When this road goes L, turn R downhill. When this lane bends L to a house, go straight on through a metal gate. Keep a straight course over the next field to a stile. Continue along a similar course in the next field but go R of a dew pond and then bear R to a stile in the R-hand hedge. In the next field head to the top L corner. Turn L and at the corner of the garden, bear R to the R edge of the field which borders a wood. At the end of the wood, turn R and then, almost immediately, L over a stile. Walk on with hedge R. Near the end, go R over one stile and then L over a second into a wood. Follow the path over two plank bridges to a stile. Bear L to go diagonally over a field to a stile near the top R corner. Go L and then bear R across the next field to a stile on the far side. This leads up steps to a stile and a field. Turn L and follow the hedge to a stile, a drive and a road. Turn L and then R along a track next to Egerton House. Follow the dirt drive along the R edge of an orchard to a gate. The path now bends R. Turn L to go along a path between the trees of an orchard to reach a gate. Walk round St James' Church to the road at Egerton. Turn R past a a shop and the George Inn. Here turn L and then R down Elm Close. At the end, take a path to R of the last bungalow. This goes around the edge of a field to a road. Turn R.

(OSL 189: OSP 1210/1230) (3.75m/6km)

51: EGERTON

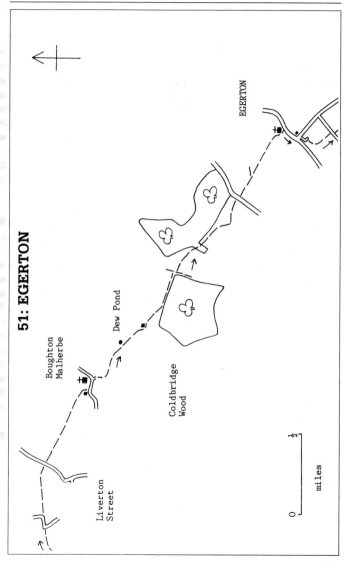

Boughton Malherbe

Dew Pond

Liverton Street

Coldbridge Wood

EGERTON

0   ½   miles

52: PLUCKLEY

After 200yds turn L into Stone Hill Farm and R down a concrete lane. Go over three stiles and along the L edge of a field to a stile. Go up steps and over a stile to a road. Turn R for 50yds and L along a permissive path at Greenhill Farm. Go through a metal gate R and over a culverted brook. Turn R over two stiles and walk on with hedge R over a small gate and the next stile to turn R through a gate to a drive. Go immediately L over a stile. Follow the hedge L over a bridge and a stile. Bear R to a stile and go diagonally over a field to farm buildings. Go through a gate and via the farm yard to another gate. Head to the R-hand corner of the field where a gate leads to a path which follows a ditch to a culvert. Cross here and walk on along the R bank. Go L through a gate and bear R uphill to R of a hill-top house near some battered pine trees. Our way goes through a gate into a fenced area and out by a stile. Bear R via a small field and a lane to a road at Pluckley. Turn L to pass a shop and a R turn (to The Black Horse). After 100yds go R into a playing field and through a gap in the far hedge. Go straight across an orchard to pass the rose gardens at Sheerland Farm, over a farm track, through a hedge and along the L edge of another orchard. The route continues to a road and then on a path alongside a wall. Go over a stile and on with fence L over two more stiles and through a gate. Keep the same course through an orchard to a farm track and a stile. Turn L and follow the L edge of an orchard to a stile in the far corner. Cross the next field towards Little Chart Church to the road at The Swan Inn. Turn R and then L over a stile opposite Gate Cottage. Bear R to cross a stile in the far corner of the field. Follow the R edge of the next field over a bridge and a stile. Cross the next field and turn R along a track. Turn L at the road into Little Chart Forstal. Two hundred and fifty yards after the last house, go L through a gate and R to a stile in the far hedge. Cross the road and take the path opposite into woods.

(OSL 189: OSP 1230) (4.5m/7.25km)

52: PLUCKLEY

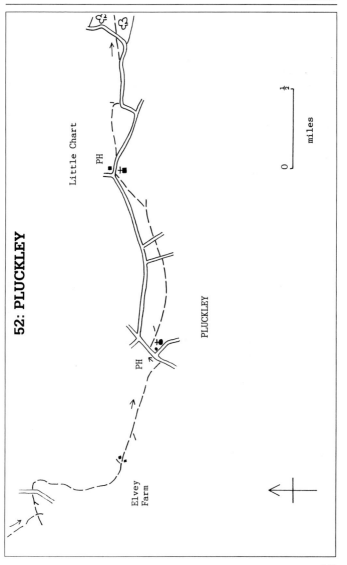

Little Chart

PH

PLUCKLEY

PH

Elvey
Farm

0

miles

53: HOTHFIELD

At a fork bear L over a footbridge. Go diagonally R with a ditch L over another footbridge to a stile into a field and a second stile into a wood. Go straight on with pond R to Hothfield Common. One hundred yards after emerging, turn R at a waymark post to another post near a nature trail post (No. 7). Fork R to a raised concrete path. At the end turn L and then, after 50yds, R over a stile. Cross a stile and then a double stile into a field. Turn L with hedge L to another double stile. Go diagonally R uphill to three more stiles. Follow the fence L and go L via a stile to a road. Turn L along the road to cross a stile R. Follow the fence to a kissing gate and cross the field towards a barn. Cross a stile and turn L to reach a gate and then a road. Go through a gate and bear L away from a metalled path to cross a stile near white gates. Go on with fence close R and bear L through a gate near a duck farm. The path goes straight on to cross a footbridge. Now bear L to the L corner. Cross the road at a T-jct and go up a path that winds around a World War II pillbox. Turn L along the edge of the field and on through woods. Cross a stile and go up the centre of the next field to a kissing gate. Cross the drive to Godington Park to another kissing gate and on to a third. Turn R to walk along the field edge. After 100yds, turn R along the edge of the next field for 200yds. Now turn R to reach a kissing gate and then continue on to a second. Bear L down to an obvious driveway. Walk straight on for $^3/_4$ mile (cross the Great Stour and the railway) to a road at Great Chart. Turn R for $^1/_3$ mile and then L opposite the church along Hillcrest. Enter a field and bear R to cross a bridge over the by-pass. Go straight on and then bear L alongside a high fence to a road. Turn R for 300yds past the quarry entrance. Thirty yards further on, turn L and walk around the L edge of the field to reach a metal gate and a stile. Cross this and turn R.

(OSL 189: OSP 1230) (5.25m/8.5km)

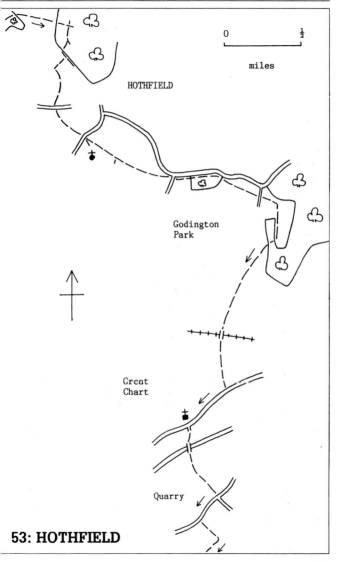

0   ½

miles

HOTHFIELD

Godington
Park

Great
Chart

Quarry

53: HOTHFIELD

And along the Saxon Shore

We're now on the final stretch with only the ancient Kentish coastland to negotiate before arriving at our journey's end at Dover. Our companion for these last few miles is the Saxon Shore Way: a waymarked long-distance footpath which follows the Kent and Sussex coast for 135 miles from Gravesend in the north to Rye in the south. We join it just to the east of Hamstreet and follow it, well most of it, along the final sections of the Southern Coast to Coast to the tercentenary plinth in the Western Docks area.

Our first chance to see the coast occurs near Adlington where, high on the chalk escarpment, we are able to look down over the flat lands of Romney Marsh to Dungeness power station and the English Channel. Romney Marsh is a strange, almost supernatural place. Criss-crossed by drainage ditches, the land here is only barely above sea level. In the days of old, this was a bleak and wild place. Before the drainage was improved, disease was rife and the area had a reputation for smugglers. Even now the bare flat pasture lands are, for some reason, a little daunting. One tends to stay at the edge and peer across rather than venture forward. Even we, intrepid explorers as we are, skirt the edges by taking a route which goes along the northern embankment of the Royal Military Canal. This northern boundary around the neck of Romney Marsh was built in the early 1800s as a defensive barrier against the threat of invasion from France. Whether a thirty-foot wide ditch would have stopped an army that had conquered most of Europe was always a matter of debate and luckily it's efficacy was never tested. The gun positions can still be determined on the ground by the periodic sideways shift of the canal. This allowed them to protect stretches of the ditch by firing along its length.

Hythe and Dover, of course, are both Cinque ports. These were originally a confederation of towns which supplied the King with a navy for odd jobs (like repelling the French) in return for certain royal privileges. There were initially just five towns (hence the name Cinq) but latterly Rye and Winchelsea joined the confederation.

Presumably nobody liked the name Sept Ports so Cinque Ports it remained. Nowadays the role is strictly ceremonial as anybody who has had to fight their way through the crowds of French school children in Rye will no doubt have realised.

The last stretch of the Southern Coast to Coast from Hythe through Sandgate and on to Folkestone is as good a prom walk as you can find. And there's plenty to see. At Hythe, steam fans will find it hard to pass the station of the Romney, Hythe & Dymchurch Railway - reputed to be the only main line train in the world to be built in miniature. Folkestone's Old Town harbour is an attractive spot and perhaps all the better for losing its cross-channel ferry traffic. Those interested in the transport of the future by the way, may wish to detour to the north of the town where the massive road ways and train lines gather themselves at the entrance to the channel tunnel. Those not so keen can use the oldest form of transport known, feet, to scale those last hills over the cliffs to Dover.

For refreshments en route it's head down from Kingsnorth all the way to Hythe. If you get desperate however, there is a pub and shop at Aldington and a CAMRA recommended pub (the Welcome Stranger) at Court-at-Street. The position of both is noted in the main text. From Hythe to Folkestone, there is a string of pubs, shops and cafes. In Sandgate the Ship Inn is CAMRA & GPG and the Clarendon Inn GPG, Folkestone has a wide range of facilities although CAMRA recommend the Clifton Hotel. In Dover, CAMRA recommend the Boars Head, the Eagle Hotel and the Royal Oak. GPG recommend the High & Dry.

54: KINGSNORTH

Walk on with the hedge to R to go through two gates to a road. Turn L to a T-jct and turn L again. Continue along the road for 200yds and cross a stile R. Walk along the farm track following the course of a fence L. Cross a stile and carry on along the track. Follow the fence as it turns L and then turn R with a ditch to L to reach a hedge. Turn L and follow this permissive path to a plank bridge out to a road. Cross to the similar bridge opposite then bear R across a field to a stile, a footbridge and a stile. Cross the lane and a stile and walk on along the R-hand edge of the field round to a footbridge and a stile into a road. Turn R and walk on to the Queen's Head pub in Kingsnorth. Cross the main road and continue along Church Hill past a small shop. Shortly after passing St Michael's and All Angels Church, turn R along a clear track. Go over a stile and walk on with the hedge to L to another stile. Head diagonally across the field aiming for a barn conversion. Cross the stile, turn R along the road for a few yards and then turn L into the farmyard. Go over the gate and walk to the top R-hand corner of the field. Go through a gate and turn R to cross a stile. Turn L to follow the edge of the wood. As this curves away L, bear R past a pole to go over a plank bridge and a stile. Continue over the derelict land to a stile which leads to Stumble Lane. Walk on to a telephone box and turn L. After 50yds, turn R along a lane. This bends R and then L and goes into Braeside Farm. Continue straight through the farm yard. At the top of the hill bear R to follow the track which now goes on for ⅓ mile to the deserted Lone Barn Farm. At the buildings, go through the gate L and go R around the pond. Now continue uphill to a stile and a gate to the L of the old farmhouse. Go straight on across the next field. Continue over gate and stile, then bear L to stile in L corner. Turn L along wood edge to stile. Bear R with railway L, over stile to gate.

(OSL 189: OSP 1230/1250/1251) (5.25m/8.5km)

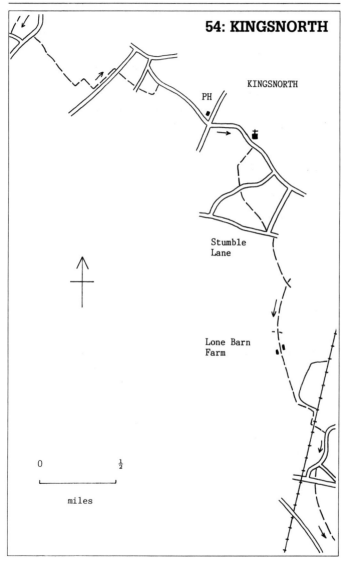

54: KINGSNORTH

KINGSNORTH

PH

Stumble
Lane

Lone Barn
Farm

0   ½

miles

55: SAXON SHORE WAY

Cross the railway and walk on to a road. Turn R. After passing a L turn, go L to cross two stiles to a road. Cross stile opposite to walk on over two fields (three stiles). The way goes via an alley and on along the L field edge. At end cross a plank bridge to road (end of Greensand Way). Turn L to T-jct and go straight on along track. When fence L goes L, turn L (by SSW waymark). The path goes through trees, over plank bridge and on between ponds to a clearing. Turn L at X-track and, after 10yds, R to take meandering route to stile and field. Go half L over the field to the corner of wood and then turn R to stile. Follow path through trees, over brook to an open area with field ahead. Bear L to fence. Turn R with fence L. When this goes L, bear R to waymark post. Now turn L to cross field, with pond R, to gate. Cross road and continue on hedged path into a wood via gate. At fork go R. After crossing a brook, bear R to follow waymarks to road. Turn L. After 400yds, turn R through gate opposite a farm entrance. Follow the L field edge over stile and on to another stile hidden by a bush. Now go downhill to the L corner to cross a fence, a stile and a brook into woods. Follow path over X-track to stile. Cross next field with hedge L to road. Turn L then R at T-jct. Just past post box, go L over stile and on with hedge L. Enter fenced off path to L and walk on, over stile to hedged path. At end cross stile L and walk on with fence R. Cross next stile and follow path L. Go over stile and on with hedge R through a white gate to drive. Follow this to pass a shed and garage and then bear R over stile. Turn L to gate and then bear L through two gates to road. Turn R to T-jct and turn L (go straight on for pub and shop in Aldington). After 100yds, go R through gate and over field to stile. Turn L to follow field edge as it goes R. Go over stile and on with fence L. Cross next stile to field and walk with woods R to stile R.

(OSL 189: OSP 1251) (5.5m/8.75km)

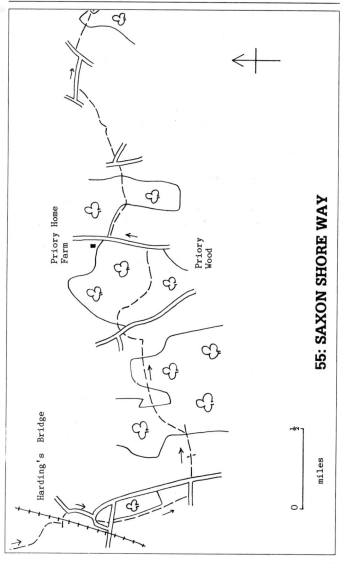

55: SAXON SHORE WAY

Priory Home Farm

Priory Wood

Harding's Bridge

miles

0

56: ROYAL MILITARY CANAL

Don't go through stile R but turn L towards power cables. Near an oak tree in the field, bear R to the hedge and go through it and on over a brook towards a pylon. Now bear L with the pylon R to go uphill towards some sheep pens. Go through a gate to the R of the pens and then L through a second gate into a field. Go straight ahead over a hurdle and on to a gate and a road. Turn R. Walk on for nearly $1/2$ mile to a road junction. Turn L and, shortly after, R down a concrete drive. This becomes a dirt drive and continues downhill through a gate and on with woods R. Continue to L of power cable pole, with views to Dungeness R, to top L corner at base of escarpment. Cross a stile and walk on along L-hand field edge. Further on cross a stile and walk on with fence R. As fence curves R, bear L to cross a stile near a gate. (If thirsty go straight on here to a road and then turn R to reach the Welcome Stranger pub at Court-at-Street.) Turn R to follow a path along the edge of a hill. On reaching an open field, the path bends R to follow the hedge R downhill. The path goes over a hurdle and at the end goes steeply down to a stile and a plank bridge. Bear R with house R to go through a gate. Turn L over a brook and L again over a hurdle to walk on the military road with the Royal Military Canal to R. This path continues for the next 2 miles with Port Lympne Wildlife Sanctuary and then Lympne Castle to L.

(OSL 189: OSP 1251/1252) (4.5m/7km)

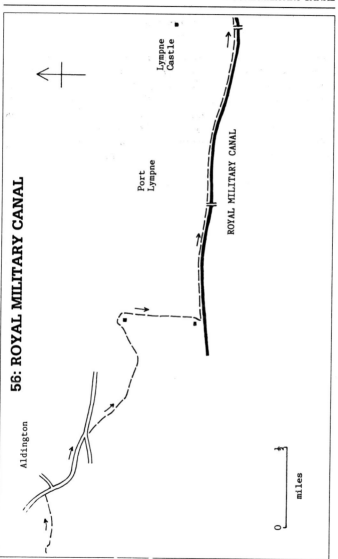

56: ROYAL MILITARY CANAL

Aldington

Port
Lympne

Lympne
Castle

ROYAL MILITARY CANAL

miles

0

57: HYTHE

The route goes on with the canal R to cross a road at West Hythe. Continue along the L-hand bank of the canal for 2 miles to reach Hythe near the station of the Romney, Hythe & Dymchurch Railway. Here the path is forced L to a parallel road which leads to traffic lights. Cross the road and turn R to cross the canal. Turn L to walk on with canal now to L. Cross the road again near The Dukes Head. Take the path to the L of the pub with the canal to L. Walk on along the R-hand bank of the canal for the next 2 miles.

(OSL 189: OSP 1252) (3.75m/6km)

57: HYTHE

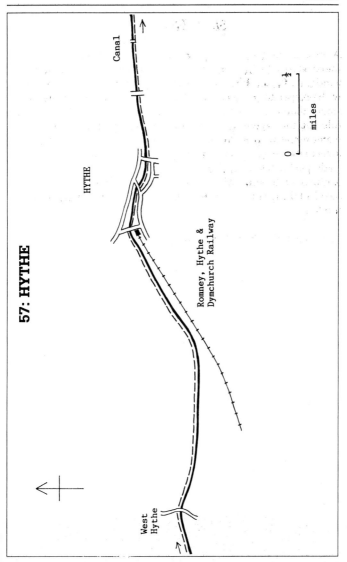

Canal

HYTHE

Romney, Hythe &
Dymchurch Railway

West
Hythe

0   ¼   ½

miles

58: SANDGATE

At its end, the canal curves R to the sea. Walk up steps and across the coast road to the promenade. Turn L to walk along the shore into Sandgate. When the road L, bears away from the shoreline, stay with promenade even though along one stretch it is so covered with stones that it is indistinguishable from the beach. (NOTE: At high tide you may prefer to go inland as at one point the height of the water forces walkers to make a 4-5ft jump down from one groyne level to the next - it's not hard but you may get your feet wet!). This leads past a castle and back on to a concrete promenade which continues into Folkestone. Pass the funicular railway L and then bear L of the Leisure Dome to walk on with an amusement park and fun fair to R.

(OSL 189: OSP 1252) (3.75m/6km)

58: SANDGATE

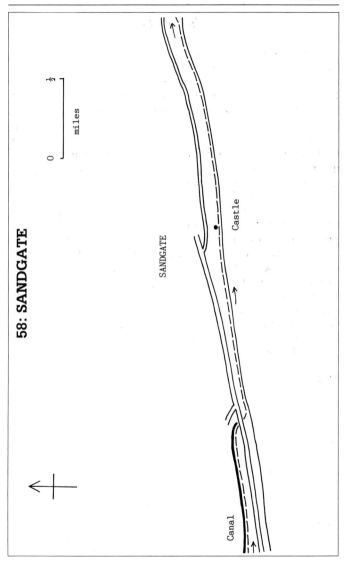

miles

0 ½

SANDGATE

Castle

Canal

59: FOLKESTONE

Walk on along the pavement with the amusement park to R. The road bends L with the (now closed) ferry terminal to R and the Hotel Burstin to L. After passing the harbour R, turn R to go past the Royal George pub and under an archway to enter the Fish Market. Walk on past the Ship Inn and along the promenade in the direction of the East Cliff Pavilion Cafe. At the end of the prom, go L up the zig-zagging steps. At the top, turn R to walk on with the cafe L. Follow the metalled path around the cliff edge with a coast guard lookout hut to L. When you reach a playing field head towards the top L-hand corner and continue along the metalled drive which goes to the L of the Martello Tower. Just past the tower, go straight on along a concrete path. This goes up, over a bridge and onto the Downs. At a cross path and footpath notice, turn R to walk up a slight slope and turn L to go under some power cables. Walk on along the top of the cliff with The Warren and the railway down the cliff to R. After going down some steps and then back up again, turn L along a concrete drive for 30yds before turning R to go up some more steps. This fenced path eventually leads back to the cliff path. Pass to L of the Cliff Top Cafe and further on, just before a large white house, turn L along a fenced path to a drive. Turn R. The drive returns the path to the cliff. When the drive ends, continue with fence to L towards Dover.

(OSL 189/179: OSP 1252) (4.75m/7.5km)

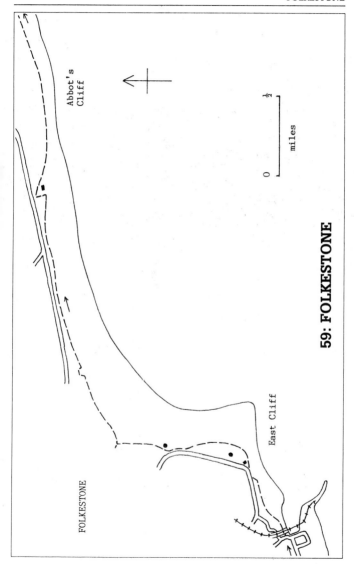

Abbot's
Cliff

miles

0

½

59: FOLKESTONE

FOLKESTONE

East Cliff

Wild sea on the Kent coast

60: DOVER

The coast path continues with increasing amounts of industry to both sides. The clear path goes downhill and then rises again staying close to the cliff edge (do not cross tempting stiles L). The route eventually descends to a concrete path with a metal fence and a cliff to R. Follow this path down to a road (the end of the North Downs Way) and turn R. The road bends L with a port area R. After crossing a railway, there is an AA building L and a turning R - Union St (if you pass the Grand Shaft you've gone too far). Turn R to walk towards the Western Docks clock tower and the entrance to the Hoverport. Go over a swing bridge into Western Docks. The walk ends in Waterloo Crescent at a plinth erected to commemorate the spot where Charles II landed to restore the monarchy on 25 May 1660. You can now restore your feet. You've made it. Well done!

(OSL 179: OSP 1252/TR 24/34) (2.75m/4.5km)

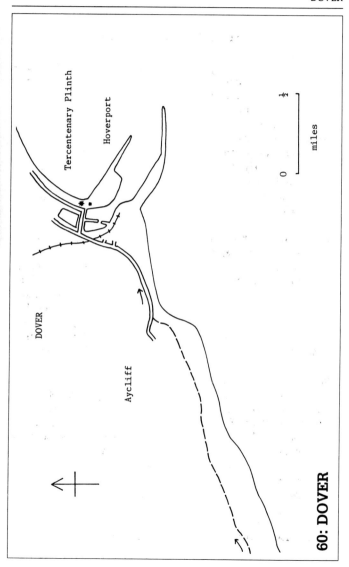

Tercentenary Plinth

Hoverport

DOVER

Aycliff

60: DOVER

0   ½

miles

APPENDIX 1: ITINERARY

The walk from Weston-super-Mare to Dover covers some 283 miles. The breakdown of such a considerable distance into suitable staging points for each day depends upon your own walking abilities and the availability of accommodation and/or public transport locally. It goes without saying that anyone undertaking such a walk needs to plan ahead. Most of the places along the way do not have extensive accommodation and what public transport exists may be comparatively rare. It is vital therefore to check the availability of either or both before setting off.

The following schedules are suggestions based on availability of accommodation and public transport.

Schedule 1: A sixteen-day plan that assumes an ability to walk about twenty miles/day.
Weston-super-Mare; Cheddar, Shepton Mallet; Warminster; Wilton; Broughton (bus to Salisbury or Winchester); New Alresford (bus to Winchester or Alton); Selborne (bus to Alton or Petersfield); Witley BR Station (train to Guildford or Haslemere); Westcott (bus to Guildford or Dorking); Bletchingly (bus to Reigate or Westerham); Sevenoaks; Linton (bus to Maidstone); Great Chart (bus to Ashford); Hythe; Dover.

Schedule 2: A twenty-three-day plan that assumes an ability to walk up to sixteen miles/day with an average of about twelve.
Weston-super-Mare; Wavering Down bus stop (bus to Cheddar or Weston) (or Shipham); Wells; Shepton Mallet; Frome; Warminster; Wylye; Salisbury; Broughton (bus to Salisbury or Winchester); Winchester; New Alresford (bus to Winchester or Alton); Selborne (bus to Alton or Petersfield); Hindhead (bus to Haslemere, Farnham, Guildford); Shamley Green (bus to Guildford or Dorking); Westcott (bus to Guildford or Dorking); Redhill; Limpsfield (bus to Reigate or Westerham); Shipbourne (bus to Maidstone); Linton (bus to Maidstone); Pluckley; Hamstreet (train to Rye or Ashford); Hythe; Dover.

For those who wish to devise their own schedule, the following chart describes the approximate mileage from Weston-super-Mare:

MILES	SECTION
0	Weston-super-Mare
8.25	Loxton
12	Wavering Down A38
13.75	Shipham
19.75	Bradley Cross (Cheddar)
22.25	Draycott
25.75	Priddy
28.5	Wookey
30.75	Wells
37.5	Shepton Mallet
46.5	Mells
50.5	Frome
59.75	Warminster
64.25	Heytesbury
72.75	Wylye
82.5	Wilton
87.25	Salisbury
91.75	Pitton
99.25	Broughton
103.25	Kings Somborne
112.75	Winchester
122.75	New Alresford
128.5	A31 near Four Marks
136.25	Selborne
141	Broxhead Common
148	Grayshott
149	Hindhead
156	Witley BR station
160.5	Hascombe
164.75	Shamley Green
171.5	Holmbury St Mary
174	Leith Hill

MILES	SECTION
178	Westcott
180	Dorking
182.75	Brockham
188	Reigate
190.25	Redhill
194.75	Bletchingly
202	Limpsfield
207	Toys Hill
212	Sevenoaks Weald
218	Shipbourne
222	West Peckham
226.75	Yalding
231.25	Linton
235.25	Sutton Valence
243	Egerton
245	Pluckley
251.75	Great Chart
254.75	Kingsnorth
261	Hamstreet
266	Royal Military Canal
270.5	Hythe
275.5	Folkestone
283	Dover

APPENDIX 2: PUBLIC TRANSPORT

For specific local transport queries, coasters should refer to the tourist information offices (see list in Appendix 3) or look up local bus companies in the appropriate Yellow Pages. These are normally available at local libraries. The following selected list of public transport was correct at the time of writing but MUST be checked before setting out.

WESTON-SUPER-MARE TO WELLS

Weston has a BR station (enquiries: 0934-621131) which connects to points south-west and to Bristol Temple Mead. Badgerline bus 126 (enquiries: 0225-464446) connects Weston with Wells via Cheddar. This bus stops on the A38 near the bottom of Wavering Down and at Draycott. Shipham is connected to Weston by the 820/821 which goes via Uphill (enquiries: 0934-621201). No buses go from Shipham to Wells.

WELLS TO SALISBURY

Wells and Frome are connected by Badgerline bus 161/162. Badgerline 184 goes from Bath to Frome via Mells. Frome and Warminster are connected by Badgerline 53 (all Badgerline enquiries: 0225-464446). Frome and Warminster have BR stations for connections to Bath/Bristol, Taunton, London and Salisbury. Upton Scudamore, Warminster, Heytesbury, Wylye (at the Deptford flyover), Wilton and Salisbury are connected via the Wilts & Dorset bus X4 (enquiries: 0722-336855). Wilton and Salisbury are also served by W&D's 60/60A/61.

SALISBURY TO WINCHESTER

Hampshire bus 32/34 runs from Salisbury to Winchester via Middle Winterslow, Broughton and Kings Somborne (enquiries: 0962-852352). Pitton and Winterslow are also served by a Hampshire bus (no. 277) as well as Bells Coaches (enquiries: 0980-862322). Both go to Salisbury.

WINCHESTER TO HINDHEAD

Winchester, New Alresford, Four Marks and Alton are connected by Alder Valley bus 214/215 or, on Sundays, County bus 453 (enquiries: 0962-852352). Selborne is connected to Alton and Petersfield by the Alder Valley bus 202 (enquiries: 0428-605757). Alton has a main line BR station for Waterloo. Hindhead is connected to Haslemere, Liphook, Broxhead Common and Alton by Alder Valley bus 213; no. 294 goes to Petersfield (all enquiries: 0428-605757).

HINDHEAD TO WESTERHAM

Alder Valley 267 goes from Hindhead to Godalming and Guildford (enquiries: 0428-605757). Witley has a BR station that connects with Haslemere and Guildford (enquiries: 0483-755905). Alder Valley bus 107 links Shamley Green with Guildford (enquiries: 0483-575226). Dorking, Westcott, Holmbury St Mary and Guildford are connected by Tillingbourne 22 (enquiries: 0483-276880) or London & Country 425/525 (enquiries: 081-668-7261). Dorking has two BR stations which connect with Guildford, Reigate and Redhill (enquiries: 0483-755905).

At Brockham Green, Tillingbourne bus 22 goes to Dorking or Guildford and Tillingbourne 547/573 goes to Dorking, Reigate and Redhill (enquiries: 0483-276880). Both Reigate and Redhill have BR stations. Redhill is on the main London to Brighton line (enquiries: 071-928-5100). London & Country bus 410 runs between Reigate and Westerham calling at South Nutfield, Bletchingly, Godstone, Oxted and Limpsfield (enquiries: 081-668-7261).

WESTERHAM TO MAIDSTONE

Although not directly on the route, it may be useful to know that Westerham and Sevenoaks are linked by Kentish bus 23 (enquiries: 0474-321300). Shipbourne connects with Tunbridge Wells and Borough Green BR stations using the Maidstone & District buses 222 and 223 (enquiries: 0634-832666). Yalding has a BR station which connects to Maidstone East for London (enquiries: 0227-454411). Bygone Buses also run from Yalding to Maidstone (enquiries: 0580-893680). Maidstone can be reached from Linton using Maidstone & District buses 4 or 5 and from Sutton Valence using bus 12 (enquiries for both: 0634-832666).

MAIDSTONE TO DOVER

Little Chart, Pluckley and Egerton are served by the East Kent bus 523 from Ashford (enquiries: 0843-581333). There is a Pluckley BR station (for trains between Ashford and Sevenoaks) (enquiries: 0227-454411); it is 1¹/₂ miles south of the village. East Kent bus 400 runs between Great Chart and Ashford (enquiries: 0843-581333). Hamstreet has a BR station which offers trains to Ashford and Hastings (enquiries: 0227-454411). Hythe, Sandgate and Folkestone are connected by East Kent buses no. 12 (enquiries: 0843-581333). Both Dover and Folkestone have BR stations (enquiries: 0227-454411).

APPENDIX 3: ACCOMMODATION

Providing an accommodation list is a tortuous and often thankless task, suggesting, as it does, a recommendation and some kind of responsibility for quality and value. With management changes, businesses coming and going, prices changing, difficulties over desired price ranges etc, I've decided not to provide specific names and addresses but to point you in the following directions.

TOURIST INFORMATION OFFICES
The ever-helpful local men and women of these offices are usually more than able to provide details of a suitably priced B&B, hotel or campsite. Their lists are as up to date and comprehensive as they can be. The appropriate telephone numbers are:

Weston-s-M	0934-750833	Cheddar:	0934-744071
Wells:	0749-672552	Frome:	0373-467271
Warminster:	0985-218548	Salisbury:	0722-334956
Winchester:	0962-840500	Alton:	0420-88448
Guildford:	0483-444007	Sevenoaks:	0732-450305
Maidstone:	0622-673581	Ashford:	0233-629165
Folkestone:	0303-58594	Dover:	0304-205108

RAMBLERS' YEARBOOK & ACCOMMODATION GUIDE
The Ramblers' Association updates its yearbook annually (believe it or not). The accommodation list is comparatively thin but nevertheless useful. The yearbook is available in bookshops and libraries but, failing this, the RA's address is:
    1/5 Wandsworth Road, London SW8 2XX.

AA/RAC/ENGLISH TOURIST BOARD etc.
These volumes are widely available through the relevant

organisations who regularly advertise in newspapers and magazines such as the Radio Times, or in bookshops (eg. W.H.Smith). HOWEVER, local libraries hold the latest editions of all these guides as well as numerous others. My local library reference section has two shelves full of various guides!

THE YOUTH HOSTEL ASSOCIATION
The YHA can provide an up-to-date list. Its address is YHA, Trevelyan House, 8 St Stephen's Hill, St Albans, Herts AL1 2DY. However, try the local library first for further information. The relevant hostels are in:

Cheddar:	0934-742494	Salisbury:	0722-327572
Winchester:	0962-853723	Hindhead:	042-860-4285
Crockham Hill		Dover:	0304-201314
(Oxted):	0732-866322		
Holmbury St M.	0306-730777		

CAMPING
A lot of campsites never reach a list but two annuals are useful: *Camping Sites in Britain* (published by Link House Magazines Ltd, Link House, Dingwall Avenue, Croydon CR9 2TA. 081-686-2599); and *Code's Camping & Touring Caravan Site Guide* (Merwain Publishing Ltd, PO Box 146, Bletchley, Milton Keynes, Bucks).

THE PLACES
For reference, the walk goes through or passes near (within 2 miles of) the following towns and villages. Large towns within commuting distance are listed in brackets.

Avon
Weston-super-Mare, Loxton, Winscombe

Somerset
Shipham, Cheddar, Draycott, Priddy, Wookey Hole, Wells, Shepton Mallet, Chelynch, Mells, Frome, (Westbury), Upton Scudamore, Warminster.

Wiltshire
Chapmanslade, Heytesbury, Codford, Stockton, Wylye, Wilton, Salisbury, Pitton, Winterslow.

Hampshire
Broughton, Houghton, Kings Somborne, (Stockbridge), (Romsey), Winchester, Itchen Abbas, New Alresford, Four Marks, (Alton), Selborne, Headley, (Liphook).

Surrey
Grayshott, Hindhead, (Haslemere), Hambledon, Hascombe, (Godalming & Guildford), Shamley Green, Westcott, Dorking, Brockham, Betchworth, Reigate, Redhill, South Nutfield, Bletchingly, Godstone, Oxted, Limpsfield.

Kent
Westerham, Toys Hill, Ide Hill, Sevenoaks, Shipbourne, West Peckham, Nettlestead, Yalding, (Maidstone), Linton, Sutton Valence, Egerton, Pluckely, Great Chart, (Ashford), Kingsnorth, Hamstreet, Hythe, Sandgate, Folkestone, Dover.

✳   ✳   ✳

PRINTED BY
CARNMOR PRINT & DESIGN, LONDON ROAD, PRESTON